Triumphs of the Heart

BOOK II

Triumphs of the Heart

BOOK II

*More Miraculous True Stories
of the Power of Love*

CHRIS BENGUHE

A Perigee Book

A Perigee Book
Published by The Berkley Publishing Group
A division of Penguin Putnam Inc.
375 Hudson Street
New York, New York 10014

Copyright © 2001 by Chris Benguhe
Book design by Tiffany Kukec
Cover design by Charles Björklund and Kiley Thompson
Cover art by Kamil Vojnar/Photonica
Author photo by Scott Foust

First edition: August 2001

Published simultaneously in Canada.

Visit our website at
www.penguinputnam.com

Library of Congress Cataloging-in-Publication Data

Benguhe, Chris.
Triumphs of the heart. Book II : more miraculous true stories of
the power of love / by Chris Benguhe.
    p. cm.
ISBN 0-399-52685-4
1. Love. I. Title.
BF575.L8 B38 2001
152.4'1—dc21   2001016316

Printed in the United States of America

10 9 8 7 6 5 4 3 2 1

To Babycat with Love

Contents

Contents

Acknowledgments

Three years ago I left my job as a reporter with the goal of making the world a better place by spreading stories of hope and love instead of tragedy and despair. And I owe a great debt of gratitude to the many people whose support and encouragement along the way helped to make that dream a reality. Though impossible to thank every voice that added to the chorus of confidence in this project I want to recognize a few here.

Thanks to all of my family, and to friends Jim DeKorse, Eric Van Drunen, Greg Moore, Scott Foust and Van and Yuki Le, because without friends, love is a lonely word. And a special thanks to Lucette Picard and Norma Storms whose heart and compassion helped to spread the word.

Once again, last but not least, thanks to my supportive

and understanding editor and friend, Jennifer Repo, my research assistant, Kathryn Pease, and to all those living and breathing beacons of hope that occupy the pages of this book. Their courage and commitment to love in the face of life's greatest challenges have already inspired so many others and hopefully will make life that much more meanignful for so many more.

Introduction

After writing the first *Triumphs of the Heart*, I spent several months traveling the country from coast to coast spreading the encouraging stories found in the pages of that book. Along the way I had the privilege of meeting so many wonderful and thoughtful people. Together we discussed the life-changing philosophies of those that made these real-life miracles happen. The result was nothing short of amazing as people from so many different places and perspectives came together to speak of how they too have been transformed by the power of love, just as I was when I first compiled these stories, which inspired me to leave my well-paying job as a tabloid reporter.

For many years as a reporter for *People* magazine, *The National Enquirer*, *The Globe* and *The National Examiner*, I covered all kinds of sensational tragedies like the O. J. Simpson story, where I was one of the first on the scene of the grisly murders, to the JonBenet Ramsey murder mystery and countless others in between. Then, finally only a month before I left my job, the Columbine story broke and changed my life forever. National media descended like vultures, trying to find out what was wrong with our schools, what was wrong with our children, our teachers and our parents, and what was wrong with Columbine. All these thousands of journalists were focusing on what was wrong. What about what was right? The truth of the matter is that despite the sadness and senselessness of what happened at Columbine, statistically school violence was down dramatically over the course of the last decade in the United States. Deranged and disturbed people will always be among us in our society, and sadly, sometimes they will be juveniles. Columbine was a heartbreaking and devastating incident, but it was not cause for the mass media hysteria that undeniably brought about a copycat shooting by a similarly deranged youth the following month at Heritage High School in Rockdale County, Georgia.

Well, the truth is that there are far more triumphs in the world each day than there are tragedies, but editors only want one victory story for every four or five tragedies. That's the formula. Open up your newspaper tomorrow and count them for yourself on the front page. As I saw society become more and more depressed by this journalistic "tragicide," I saw that there were hundreds of uplifting and incredibly dramatic stories that go unwritten every day involving people who have overcome life's greatest obstacles to achieve happiness for themselves and their loved ones. That's why I quit my lucrative job and began writing these important collections of "triumphs of the heart."

As I interviewed the people behind these positive and amazing stories of victory over tragedy, I made yet another incredible discovery: The subjects of these stories knew that no matter how much tragedy they read about in the papers and more importantly whatever very real hardships existed in their own lives, it could all be overcome with a real and active love. These are people who made miracles happen not by chance or divine intervention but because of the life-changing and life-saving power of devotion and kindness. It's the love of family and friends, of humanity. The people in *Triumphs of the Heart, Book II* all faced adversity at some point in their lives, sometimes more than once. But they eventually realized that they had the capacity to love others and to be loved themselves, even as their lives were plagued with troubles. And it is this powerful love that made it possible for hardships to be overcome. The truth I have learned is that once we realize that love is a real force in our lives and that we have the capacity to give it to others, everything else is secondary.

Enjoy these stories and be inspired by their message, then spread the message to everyone you know. Armed with the power of love, perhaps we can stop filling the world with bad news and instead fill it up with triumphs of the heart!

Spread the Love!
Christopher Benguhe
April 2001

her heart she knew it was too late. Their precious child was gone.

Sharon screamed at the top of her lungs for her husband. Gene rushed into the room and began performing CPR on the lifeless baby while Sharon and her sister frantically called for an ambulance. But nothing could be done.

"As soon as I realized what happened, I wanted to die myself," remembers Sharon. "But I knew I had to live for my husband and for the future." Sharon found strength in the memory of how her mother endured the pain when she lost her child because she knew she had to be there for the rest of her family. That gave Sharon the courage to go on.

And now her mother was right there by her side to hold her and help Sharon get past the hurt and move on. When the pain grew unbearable Sharon would rest her weary head in her mother's lap and cry like a baby. Her mother gently stroked her hair with her hands and assured her that though she would never forget, the pain would heal. And that made all the difference because Sharon knew her mother had been through this. With her support, Sharon overcame the tragedy and got back on her feet.

Still mourning, but ever hopeful for a family, the couple decided the best way to move on was to give their love to another child. And a year later their next child came into the world on the Fourth of July, 1976. But fate was against Sharon and Gene. Five months after their son Christopher was born, he had a seizure on Christmas Day. Sharon was terrified! Could the unthinkable tragedy be happening again? "I walked into the room and his whole body was limp," reveals Sharon. "It was like a nightmare. I said, this can't be happening again." But Sharon was spared more grief as her son opened his eyes and cried. This time it wasn't SIDS, but Christopher was diagnosed with a rare condition that brought on occasional seizures. Medication allowed him to live a relatively normal and healthy life, and another child, Gabriel, was born healthy four years later.

Sharon moved on with her life, but just as her mother predicted she never could forget the death of her first child. Like most parents who suffer the devastating experience of SIDS, though she knew her baby's death wasn't her fault, she never stopped blaming herself for what happened and wished that there was something she could have done to save her. "I knew rationally that her death was beyond my control," says Sharon. "But I just couldn't seem to close that chapter completely in my heart."

A few years later when times grew tight for their family, Sharon decided to take a part-time job to help out. She waitressed for a year then decided she wanted to do something a little more meaningful. When a friend told her of an opening working as a local 911 dispatcher, it was just what she was looking for. "I wanted to do something where I could help people," says Sharon. "I was brought up to always try to lead a good life and help out. But after losing my baby I guess I wanted to do that even more with my life."

Sharon applied and immediately got the job. Now only five years after her own baby died, Sharon was handling life-and-death calls and more than a few were from frantic mothers who had emergencies with their children. It was the toughest part of the job for Sharon. Whenever she'd get one of those calls her voice would change, and Sharon's fellow employees would know just from her reaction that there was a mother on the line with a child who had stopped breathing or had some other terrible accident. And every time, Sharon was determined to save them.

Sharon couldn't save all those babies, but when she saved one it was like a little more of the pain had been lifted from her heart. "At least I was making sure that one mother never had to feel what I experienced," says Sharon. "That made me feel pretty good inside."

Sharon worked hard at that job for twenty years and saved countless lives along the way because of her calm, careful and caring assistance. Then one cold winter afternoon in January, Sharon was all by herself in the dispatch center when she received an emergency call that a baby had stopped breathing—a five-week-old baby—the same age as the one Sharon had lost years earlier. It was up to Sharon to help save her. "I got a lump in my throat the moment I heard the age," remembers Sharon. "But I knew I had a job to do so I took a deep breath and did what I had to do."

The caller on the other end was Laura, a day-care center owner who'd been caring for kids as many years as Sharon had been saving lives. Laura knew CPR but she had never been tested like this before. "When that child stopped breathing I kind of froze up a little," says Laura. "I honestly didn't know if I was going to be able to get through this." But Sharon wasn't going to let her fail. She calmly walked her through all the necessary questions to assess the child's condition—most importantly to try and determine if there was a pulse. There wasn't! "When Laura told me that there was no pulse and no breathing and the baby was so still, it brought back all those memories," reveals Sharon. "But I couldn't let that affect me. Now I had to focus on helping Laura to save that baby. I didn't want her to ever feel that pain like I felt."

Sharon immediately reminded Laura how to perform CPR on the baby. While Laura began chest compressions, Sharon glanced at the address of the caller so she could send paramedics to the rescue. And something looked familiar. "The street name seemed to ring a bell," says Sharon. "But I was occupied with the call so I didn't think about it again." When Laura finished one cycle of the CPR and there was no response, she grew more frantic. But

Sharon steadied Laura enough to focus on what she had to do despite fighting her own emotions. "Sharon wouldn't give up," says Laura. "She stayed right with me and believed in me. She was like my guardian angel there to help me."

Then it happened. Just as paramedics burst in the door, the baby came back to life. Laura screamed to Sharon. "He's breathing! He's breathing!" Sharon collapsed back in her chair and let out a loud sigh. As she hung up the phone, Sharon glanced down at the screen again at the familiar address of the caller. Suddenly it hit her like a ton of bricks why it looked so familiar. It was her old house! It was the same house where she lost her own baby twenty-five years earlier. Chills ran down her spine. "I was speechless," says Sharon. "I couldn't believe this was happening." But Sharon couldn't deny it. This was real, and she felt that it couldn't just be a coincidence.

Sharon called her husband and then double-checked the woman's name and the address. Sure enough it was the very same woman they sold their house to twenty-five years earlier after losing their child. "I knew then that this was life's way of telling me that I was OK," says Sharon. "Now I could really get past what happened back then." Somehow saving this baby gave Sharon the closure she sought for so many years.

"I know it sounds crazy, but I believe that my little baby

Nikki was looking down on me and helped me save that child," says Sharon. "And I know that wherever Nikki is, now she's smiling because of it. And from now on whenever I think of her that's how I'll see her."

Adopting a Policy of Love

~⁓~

*D*onna and her mother were more than just close, they were like best friends. So when her mom's life was cut short by a massive heart attack after Donna's thirty-ninth birthday, it was a real blow to the Texas woman. After her mother's death, she had a void in her life that even her loving Baptist-minister husband couldn't fill. "I came from a big family of seventeen kids and my mother was always there taking care of us," says Donna. "I was thinking a lot about that when I heard a voice that said 'adopt.'"

When she told her husband, W. C., of her desire to adopt children he couldn't have agreed more since he, too, came from a family of many children himself. And if there was a way for his wife to cure the pain of her loss by helping an abandoned child, the minister was all for it. "My wife was hit hard by the loss of her mother, and I was there for her comfort, but she clearly needed someone else she could love," says W. C. "With so many children needing homes, adoption seemed a worthwhile alternative." Though they already had two children, a seventeen-year-old boy and an eleven-year-old girl, the minister and his wife knew there was plenty of room in their home and hearts for more children. But they never could have imagined just how big their family was going to grow.

They registered with the state of Texas to adopt and then signed up for the mandatory parenting classes. Each week Donna made the long drive from the remote Piney Back Woods of deep east Texas where she and her husband lived to the nearest city to take the classes. And she even got her divorced sister to come along and think about adopting herself. "I told her she needed another daughter," remembers Donna. "And she said she'd come with me and check it out."

Six months later W. C. and his wife adopted not one, but two children, and Donna's sister adopted a six-year-old boy herself. "These children changed our lives the moment they stepped into our home," says W. C. "They had experienced horrors at their young ages that we cannot even imagine." Now the minister and his wife had a chance to give these children a home and a life worth living. They were now the proud new parents of a little girl, Maria, 5, and a boy, Brent, 3. Maria was recently rescued from a home where she had been sexually abused, and incredibly, little Brent was so neglected he was found wandering the streets looking for food in garbage cans. Now they were both safe for the first time in their lives. "When you look into these children's eyes, it's inconceivable that anyone could hurt them," says the minister. "It was the first time in their young lives that they didn't have to be afraid. To see the smiles of happiness and security on their faces was such a joy. We knew that we were meant to adopt them."

When the minister introduced his new children to his congregation of just under 200 people, the small community welcomed them with open arms. In fact, several of the members even approached W. C. after services to ask how they too could help children who had been through such pain. W. C. had never preached to any of them that they should adopt, but it happened anyway.

As the minister marveled at the two tiny flowers that were blooming before him, they transformed from frightened and maladjusted children to happy and healthy kids, and more and more parents began asking him how they could adopt. At first the minister referred all those interested to the state agency for adoption, but when many of the willing parents explained that they couldn't afford to take time off from work or didn't have the transportation needed for the long trip to the big city to take the adoption class, W. C. had another idea. He asked the state agency to come to them. "Some of these people didn't have the money to go into the city," declares W. C. "But they had the love they needed to raise a child."

The CPS (Child Protective Services) told W. C. that if he could find at least ten sets of parents who wanted to adopt, it would send someone to the tiny community to teach the class. That next Sunday W. C. made the announcement during services that all interested parents should attend a meeting. Twenty-three sets of parents showed up. "This was phenomenonal," says a supervisor with the local child protective services. "We had never come across any single group that would adopt this many children." And with nearby Houston home to nearly 700 homeless children, W. C.'s congregation seemed like it could be the answer to a whole lot of prayers. So the CPS not only offered to teach the parenting class in the tiny town but opened a branch of the CPS right in the middle of the community. And then the caring people from the tiny church congregation came in droves.

Over the next year almost thirty-nine children were adopted by dozens of families in the small town. And within two years that number doubled again to a whopping eighty children and still that number continued to grow! It was a phenomenon of caring that was unprecedented. Finally almost one hundred forgotten children were now living happy lives with loving families. "It was a yearning and hunger within all of us to put some life into somebody else," says the minister of his congregation's motivations. "We knew what God wanted us to do. It was to help and love these children who had never known love."

As the wildfire of love spread, so did the startling stories of how lives were transformed. One family adopted five children. Another family gave refuge to a child rescued from an inner-city nightmare where he ran and hid every night from drive-by shootings. Others had been beaten and raped. And all of them had been emotionally abused or neglected in some way. But now every child was given a new lease on life thanks to the match lit by the minister and his wife.

"God put us here to love each other and to lead by example," says the minister. "My wife's desire to have a child to love inspired us to help these kids. Now we are going to love them and teach them respect for life and others so they can grow up to spread that word to everyone whose lives they touch."

A Heart Way to Learn about Love

~❧~

*A*dam was a perfectly happy and healthy thirteen-year-old boy growing up in the New Jersey suburbs in the summer of 1995, when one day he came in from the family pool complaining of a stomachache. A week later he was so violently ill that his mother rushed him to the nearest hospital emergency room. There she was shocked and stupefied when doctors informed her that her son would die unless he received a heart transplant. "It was totally unbelievable," says his mother, Maryann. "I was sure the doctor was confusing him with another patient. I kept saying, 'Are you sure you are talking about our son Adam?' It was impossible. I brought him in because he was vomiting so badly. I figured he was dehydrated."

But unfortunately the diagnosis was correct. The doctors

explained that some unknown virus had somehow entered Adam's system and made its way into his heart, destroying his left ventricle. The damage was irreversible and a heart transplant was the only option. "It all happened so fast we didn't know what to do or think," says Maryann. "But I knew my son was not going to die. We weren't going to let that happen. I truly knew in my heart that with our support and love he was going to live."

Maryann knew better than most how important the support of family is in times of tragedy. Life threw her its first curve when she was only eight years old and her mother had a massive stroke that left her completely paralyzed and barely able to speak. While her father worked, Maryann took care of her mother and successfully nursed her back from the brink to the point where she was at least able to communicate with her family. The bond of love that developed between mother and daughter is what gave her the strength to keep going over a decade later when her first husband was killed in an automobile accident while she was in labor with her first son, Mark. Then two months later her father died. "Despite her condition my mom was always there for me," remembers Maryann. "She was my biggest cheerleader. She used to say whatever didn't kill me made me stronger." Now Maryann knew she needed to pass that strength in the face of terrible adversity on to Adam.

Doctors told her that medication might keep Adam alive

for a few weeks while they searched for an available heart, but they were quick to point out that healthy hearts weren't hanging on trees. "The doctors kept telling me the odds were low that he probably wouldn't make it long enough to get a heart," says Maryann. "But I wouldn't believe that, and I didn't want them telling Adam that either. I told the doctor, 'Adam is going to be OK. God has never deserted me and he never will.'"

Adam was released from the hospital and sent home on the lifesaving medication that would hopefully keep him alive until a heart could be found. But a week later he was rushed back into the intensive care unit at Mt. Sinai Hospital in New York City. He didn't have much time left. He had lost almost sixty pounds and was as white as a ghost. Remembers Maryann, "My husband and I made a commitment to each other and then to Adam that no matter what, we were going to see him through this and he would be alright. We knew that was the most important thing we could tell him." His parents' conviction helped convince Adam that he would survive his ordeal and gave him the strength to keep holding on while the search for a heart continued.

Meanwhile his parents put their words of support into action. Maryann spent every waking moment thinking up ways to inspire and encourage her son. When her son told her how much he was craving pizza and hot dogs instead of the bland hospital food, she hit the streets of New York in search of the city's best pizza and hot dogs. "I think I checked out every pizza parlor in New York," remembers Maryann. "I practically set up a hot dog stand in his room." And mom and son spent hour after hour sharing their thoughts and emotions like never before. "We really got to know each other during those talks," remembers Maryann. "I realized he wasn't a child anymore. He had grown into a deep and beautiful young man." Alone in that hospital room with each other, mother and son became each other's confidants.

Maryann and her husband made Adam's sterile hospital room as warm and cozy as possible. They filled it with his favorite posters and games. They even made some of the intimidating hospital equipment into props for makeshift games they'd play with him. But most surprisingly, they asked Adam not to think about his own dilemma and instead to be a cheery inspiration to others. "We told him he needed to give up the burden of his illness and stop thinking about it," says Maryann. "He was a caring and concerned child by nature anyway, so we told him to remember others worse off than him. We knew what we were telling him wasn't easy considering how sick he was, but we knew he had to get his mind off his illness."

Adam responded immediately to his parents' words of wisdom and he began taking an interest in the sick babies in the hospital. And soon, despite doctor's orders to stay put, he was forcing himself out of his hospital bed every day to visit them and cheer them up. "He was a real champ," says his mom. "He was so focused on them instead of himself."

Bolstered by his parents' support and the inspiration of helping others, Adam grew stronger day by day in spirit and so did his confidence that he would live. At one point he even asked his mother to tell the doctor to "lighten up," prompting Maryann to tell the doctor to stop all the gloomy talk about any possibility that he wasn't going to make it. When the doctor tried to explain that he was only trying to be fair and realistic with Adam, she insisted that he never again tell her son that he might die.

Then came a truly unexpected boost to Adam's morale when famed director Steven Spielberg, who was starting a children's program at the hospital, asked if he could schedule a time to come visit Adam. Ironically, the night before his visit with the director, Adam had an incredible dream that easily could have been a scene in one of the director's inspiring fantasy films.

As he drifted into dreamworld, Adam suddenly saw himself on an operating table surrounded by surgeons putting in his new heart. The black-and-white dream was vivid in detail right down to a *Far Side* calendar on the wall, which read November 21. He woke up the next morning excited to tell his mom he knew that the dream would come true. "He was absolutely certain beyond a doubt that this was going to happen," remembers Maryann. "I didn't want him to get hurt if it didn't happen, but I had faith in my son, so I never told him that it was silly or wouldn't happen." And as Steven Spielberg arrived for his visit with Adam that morning it only further helped to convince him that anything was possible.

The date Adam dreamed was still two weeks away, and even if his dream did come true he still had to survive until then. But with each day Adam seemed to grow stronger, encouraged by his parents' faith in his dream although many of the medical personnel rejected it as dangerously optimistic. When the fateful day finally arrived, Adam arose with a renewed sense of spirit and confidence. "He said, 'Mom, today's the day I get my heart.' He was absolutely sure of it. He said it might not happen until around midnight, but that it was definitely going to happen." And Maryann never tried to talk him out of it. He was so sure of it, she started to really believe it might happen.

At one P.M. on November 21, Maryann was washing her son's hair when the transplant coordinator burst into their room gasping. They had found a heart for Adam! She said, "I can't believe I am telling you this. I can't believe this is really happening. But we have a heart." An eleven-year-old boy from New Jersey had been killed in an automobile accident and his parents were donating the heart. It was a perfect match. "Adam wasn't even surprised," says Maryann. "He knew it all the time. And I was so glad I never doubted him or told him not to believe in his dream."

Doctors prepared the heart and Adam for surgery. Strangely enough, as they wheeled Adam into the operating room, he recognized everything in the room from his dream, and incredibly the clock on the wall read ten minutes to midnight. Everything was just as he had predicted. Maryann couldn't help but be happily stunned by the whole experience especially her son's eerie premonition that it might not happen until midnight.

While surgeons worked, she and her husband prayed and hoped. Several hours later those prayers were answered when Adam was wheeled out of the operating room with a new, healthy, beating heart. "We knew down deep it was going to be a success," says Maryann. "But we were sure glad when it was over."

Since then Adam has been a model patient, his heart showing no rejection whatsoever. And now the college freshman has decided he wants to devote his life to helping sick children in hospitals as a child psychologist. "My parents were there to fill my head and heart with love and positive thoughts," says Adam. "I believe that's what kept me alive. Now I want to be able to give that back to other kids."

Meanwhile Maryann couldn't be more proud of her son and more thankful to those who helped her overcome her own tragedies so that she could be there for Adam. "Life is just a whisper," says Maryann. "It's that fragile and love makes all the difference."

Heroes Need Heroes Too

*J*im became a lifeguard in 1961 when a prank landed the fair-haired Los Angeles sixteen-year-old in hot water after he and some friends stole a couple of surfboards from a lifeguard station. Their youthful mischief didn't get very far before they were nabbed by lifeguards who turned them over to the police. But rather than press charges, the police offered them a deal. If they helped out the lifeguards by working for six weeks during the summer for free they'd let them off.

So Jim and the rest of the boys spent the summer doing whatever was asked of them by the lifeguards, mostly running errands and cleaning up. But when Jim witnessed one of the lifeguards saving a little boy's life, something changed inside of him. He realized he wanted to be a lifeguard, too. "That boy would have drowned," remembers Jim. "But because that lifeguard was there and devoted to doing his job well, that boy lived. I wanted to help people like that. I wanted to make my life mean something more than just hanging out on the beach meeting girls."

When the six weeks of his mandatory service was over, Jim asked to become a lifeguard and began the strenuous training to pass the rigorous test. A good swimmer and cross-country runner at school, he was already in great shape, but he still worked hard to be ready. He passed the test with flying colors and was certified to be a lifeguard. "That was one of the happiest days of my life," says Jim. "I still remember coming home with that certification paper and showing off to all my friends."

The dedicated teen worked weekends during the school year then full-time in the summer. But even when he wasn't working Jim hung out with lifeguards helping out however he could. He liked all the people he got to meet while working. The beach and the lifeguard tower became like his home away from home. But most important, Jim knew he was doing something important.

Within his first month on the job Jim pulled a dozen people to safety from dangerous riptides with his quick thinking and lightning-fast speed in the water. "I was good because I loved it," says Jim. "The concept of saving people seemed so natural. And I guess in the back of my mind I always had the fantasy of saving some beautiful girl and then she would fall in love with me forever. Truth be told there was a little of that thinking going on, too!"

Jim's damsel in distress finally showed up in January of the next year when he was actually off duty just walking on the beach, only she wasn't exactly what he was dreaming about. "I saw this elderly woman get knocked over by this enormous wave, and then I didn't see her again," recalls Jim. "I figured she either was tied up in some seaweed or caught up in an undertow. Either way I knew she needed help."

Jim kicked off his shoes and shirt and dove right in. Quick-swimming Jim located the woman in seconds and pulled her up to the surface. She was alive but had passed out when the mighty wave took her under. He immediately dragged her to the shore and revived her. "I got the water out of her lungs and then she started breathing alright," explains Jim. "She was pretty shaken though."

After carrying the woman back to the lifeguard station, an ambulance brought her to the hospital where she was examined and then released. A week later the elderly lady whose name was Victoria called to thank him. Jim was glad to have been of service. "It felt good helping her," says Jim. "That was all the reward I needed, but it was nice to get the call."

What Jim didn't realize was that she would be calling again and again and again to check up on him over the next few months. She even started ordering him pizzas when she knew he was going to be at work. The rest of the guys started joking with Jim about the "older woman" in his life. But Jim didn't mind the jokes, and he liked talking to his new friend.

Jim graduated that year from high school and decided to stay on as a lifeguard while he took classes at a nearby community college. Meanwhile the kind calls and gestures from his adoring older woman kept coming, and Jim reciprocated whenever he had a chance by calling to say hi. He even dropped by her place every once in a while for a soda or to sit and talk for a minute.

They kept up their friendship for the next several years, and then Jim went away for a summer trip. When he returned, he called Victoria to ask if he could drop by and bring her a gift he had for her. But someone else answered. It was the older woman's niece, Barbara. Victoria had suffered a massive stroke and died. "It hit me harder than I thought it would," remembers Jim. "In a way I wished I was there when it happened so I could have saved her. I knew there was probably nothing that I could have done. But just the same I knew then how much I loved her and how much I was going to miss her." Since Victoria had no children of her own, twenty-three-year-old Barbara had temporarily moved down from San Francisco to wrap up all her aunt's important matters. Barbara knew all about Jim and thanked him for how he had been a friend to her aunt. Jim hung up the phone and thought that he would never speak to the niece again.

Jim graduated college and kept life-guarding part-time while he pursued a career as an actor. He never became famous, and he wasn't making a whole lot of money but he was happy and having fun. Everything was fine until one night when a beach party turned deadly and Jim got into trouble. "There was a lot of drinking and drugs going on at this party, and I just wanted to get out of there," explains Jim. "So I got up and left in a hurry." But Jim didn't realize that at the same time that he left the party so did a woman he had met earlier in the evening. When she turned up missing, Jim was charged with murder! "I thought I was trapped in some kind of nightmare," remembers Jim. "I didn't even know the woman. But the next thing I knew the police were at my door arresting me." It was like some scene out of a movie for Jim, but when they slapped on the cuffs it was all too real.

The police charged Jim with the murder of the woman who they presumed was dead based on her disappearance and finding her tattered dress on the side of the road. "It was a crazy accusation," says Jim. "They didn't even have a body and I had absolutely no connection to her whatsoever except for being at the same party with her that night." But for the police a victim needed a suspect and Jim was it.

Worse still, Jim didn't have a criminal attorney or even know one. He only had an entertainment attorney who politely charged him to tell him he couldn't do anything before referring him to a pricey, high-powered defense attorney whom Jim couldn't afford. A public defender took the case while Jim tried to figure out what to do. Jim pleaded not guilty and bail was set at one hundred thousand dollars—something that was completely out of reach for Jim. Now he not only couldn't properly defend himself, he couldn't even get out of jail long enough to find someone who would. "The situation looked bleak to says the least," says Jim. "I knew that if I didn't get some help soon I was going down for this. I knew I was innocent, but nobody else seemed to care. They just all wanted to get the case over with."

But while Jim festered in jail, somebody else did care and was ready to help after reading about his situation in the paper. That somebody was Barbara—the elderly woman's niece who had been grateful to young Jim two decades earlier. Barbara was now a lawyer and had just recently left her job as a prosecuting attorney in Iowa and moved back to her hometown of San Francisco to open up her own practice as a criminal defense attorney. When she read Jim's story she knew he was innocent. "Of course I needed to hear all the facts directly from him," remembers Barbara. "But there was something about him, about how kind and loving he was when I spoke to him twenty years earlier that told me that he couldn't have done this. I wanted to help him the same way he had helped my aunt."

Barbara wrote him a letter requesting to come see him and offering to defend him simply for the cost of expenses. When Jim got the letter it was a surprise to say the least. "I felt like I was in the middle of a storm and then the sky opened up and there she was," says Jim. "She was an angel. The second I read her letter I felt like it was going to be all right, I don't know why."

Jim immediately contacted her and accepted her offer. A few days later she arrived. And the moment she saw Jim and reviewed the basic evidence of the case she knew something didn't add up. Accounts of Jim being seen with the woman who was now presumed dead didn't make sense. An eyewitness identified Jim as the man who left the party with the woman, but in his statement to police, the witness described the woman and man to be about the same height. Because the alleged dead woman was five-feet-four inches tall and Jim was almost six feet tall, Barbara knew this was impossible. "Something was very wrong with that eyewitness," remembers Barbara. "And this is what they were resting the majority of their case on. It was a total miscarriage of justice."

Barbara worked feverishly to show the court how preposterous the accusation was and was even able to get Jim's bail reduced on the basis of several crafty motions so he could be released pending the trial. After a month in prison that was a gift in itself. "I really wasn't doing well emotionally behind bars, and I was getting ready to just give up trying," admits Jim. Once out of jail Jim's spirits lifted, and he became actively involved in his own defense.

Now Barbara and Jim worked tirelessly together to disprove every one of the prosecution's assertions. Meanwhile Barbara hired a detective to uncover everything he could about the alleged victim and anything that would tie her to Jim. He found nothing related to Jim, but in the course of that investigation the detective did make the startling discovery that the dead woman was alive! She was living in Mexico at a fleabag motel under an assumed name with the man she'd been cheating on her husband with—the same man with whom she had left the party, and who was the spitting image of Jim.

"I was totally blown away when he showed me the pictures of her and this guy down in Mexico," recalls Barbara. "The woman wasn't even dead and Jim was facing life in prison. It was absolutely crazy." The incredible discovery was the product of a coincidence. The investigator Barbara had hired was good friends with the owner of the hotel where the woman was staying and during a routine conversation the subject turned to what the investigator was working on. Suddenly the innkeeper began to think about his new guest from Los Angeles and how her description fit perfectly with the missing woman.

When Barbara told Jim the news, needless to say he

was overcome with joy. "I just about died of relief," remembers Jim. "I figured that was it. I was off the hook." But as Barbara explained he wasn't out of the woods yet. They would first have to prove beyond a shadow of a doubt that this was the same woman. And across the border it would not be that easy. "As crazy as it sounds if I couldn't prove she was alive, Jim could still be tried for her murder," explains Barbara. "So I had to get real proof that this woman was definitely the alleged victim."

Barbara sent the investigator down to Mexico again to retrieve as much information as possible to make a case. He returned with more than Barbara ever could have wished for. He finally convinced the woman to return and tell the police she was, in fact, alive. Police immediately dismissed the case and released Jim.

As far as Jim was concerned, Barbara was a saint. "I spent years of my own life saving lives, but I never thought about what it would feel like to have my own neck saved," declares Jim. "It felt pretty good."

These days Jim is happier than he's ever been and lives with his wife and three children in Wyoming where he farms and runs his own small manufacturing company. But he'll never forget his very special relationship with the "older woman." "If that sweet old woman didn't talk me up to her niece the way she did I might have rotted in jail for the rest of my life," says Jim. "I owe that woman my life."

But close friend Barbara who still practices law sees Jim's good fortune a little bit differently. Says Barbara, "He saw fit to save somebody's life who he didn't even know, and he wasn't even on the job at the time. That kind of love of humanity does not go unrewarded. He deserved my help and he'd get it again in an instant."

A Lifetime of Love

~~~

*L*orenzo was delivered by a fireman in 1953 just outside Los Angeles, California, to talented, but poor, Mexican immigrant entertainers. It was just the beginning of a very special lifetime of lifesaving events that go beyond imagination.

Lorenzo's father, Luiz, and mother, Maria, were celebrated Mexican singers and dancers in their native country, but after moving to America with their children, the family was too poor to even afford medical care when Maria became pregnant with Lorenzo. "We just plain didn't have the money," says Lorenzo. "My parents worked hard and long hours at menial jobs and then worked after hours as entertainers. But the pay was so low for immigrants back then and there was no insurance."

Barely able to afford to put food on the table let alone afford doctors and hospitals, when Maria went into labor, Lorenzo's father ran to the firehouse behind their house and summoned help. Without hesitation the concerned and caring firefighters rushed to Maria's side and delivered her baby. "If it wasn't for them," says Lorenzo, "I might not even be alive today." Then just a few months later, again it was the courageous firemen who spared their lives when they woke the sleeping family after a horrible fire ravaged their tiny cottage home in the middle of the night. Lorenzo and his family narrowly escaped death as firefighters carried them out of the blazing inferno. "They were our guardian angels," recalls Lorenzo. "There was no way we would have survived if it wasn't for them."

Now homeless, the family came to depend on the kindness of others—this time friends in the community who offered them shelter until they were finally able to afford a new place to live. Along with his one older brother and two elder sisters, Lorenzo and his family worked hard at carrying on the family tradition of singing and dancing as they struggled to pay the bills and get by as best as they could. "I saw how tough it was for my parents," remembers Lorenzo. "But no matter how difficult it was for them, they always took care of us and made sure we were happy."

Yet no matter how hard Lorenzo's parents worked they could never seem to catch up with all the bills. But whenever the cold realities of their hard life became too hard to handle, Lorenzo's talented and compassionate father knew one remedy for poverty which he could always afford. He'd take out his guitar and write a song for Lorenzo, then sing it to his precious child. "That was worth all the money in the world to me," says Lorenzo. "We didn't have much, but we had plenty of love."

Incredibly when Lorenzo was just seven years old, fire would once again play a major role in his life when a blaze raged through his best friends' house. Lorenzo watched as firefighters valiantly fought a losing battle, and looked on in horror as the frustrated firemen carried the tiny, dead bodies of his friends out of the incinerated house. Then he saw the agony of the firefighters when they realized there was nothing they could do to save his friends. "As I stood there crying for my friends, I looked up for a second at this big strong fireman's face and I saw tears streaming down his cheeks," remembers Lorenzo vividly. "Then he prayed to God to bring them back to life. That's when I realized for the first time that firemen were not just doing a job—they really cared. They became my heroes."

Lorenzo grew up with the same trials and tribulations as other youths only more so because of his family's poverty and the undeniable immigrant discrimination. The tough streets of the barrio were plagued by gangs, which Lorenzo avoided at all costs. And that opposition brought harassment and threats. "I didn't want anything to do with them because my parents taught me well," says Lorenzo. "But it was impossible to avoid them. You were either with them or they were against you." The harassment grew violent one day when he was attacked on the way home from baseball practice. As he walked his devoted dog, Duke, the mob of heartless hoodlums stoned the dog to death and left Lorenzo in a pool of blood, bruises and tears.

But despite all the tragedy and hardship of his youth, Lorenzo grew up happy and healthy with his family's never-ending love and support. When it came time for him to pick a career for himself he knew what he wanted to do. He wanted to be a fireman. "I always remembered what those firefighters had done for us," reveals Lorenzo. "And I never forgot the firefighter with the tears in his eyes."

Indeed that lifesaving love led Lorenzo to sign up with the Santa Ana Fire Department many years later where he immediately began to save so many lives that he was continually recognized and awarded for his bravery by local, state, and national agencies. Now Lorenzo was the hero.

Then one night in the fall of 1990 he was putting in a long night of overtime hours when a call came over the radio that a small fire had broken out in a local tire store around the corner. But Lorenzo knew it was going to be trouble. "When I heard it was a tire fire I knew there was the potential for something big," remembers Lorenzo. "That rubber goes up fast." Lorenzo and the rest of the crew rushed to the scene, but by the time they arrived thick, black, billowing clouds of tire smoke filled the sky, and the fire was out of control. Lorenzo immediately went to work cutting giant holes in the side of the building for ventilation while his fellow firemen forged inside to try and douse the ferocious flames.

"This was one of the worst fires I'd ever seen," says Lorenzo. "And it was clear that this might be a losing battle." As the flames grew more uncontrollable, the captain made the decision to pull the men out because the fire was too far gone and too dangerous. After the order came to withdraw, Lorenzo ripped off his cumbersome gear to catch his breath and prepared to pull in the hoses. But just then, Lorenzo felt a wave of incredible heat coming his way. As he turned to see what was happening, he watched in horror as a wall of the burning building came crashing down on five firefighters sending flames high into the night sky and engulfing the whole area. "I could feel the rush of hot wind on my face even from a distance," remembers Lorenzo. "I knew the men were in there but suddenly I couldn't see them through the smoke. I had to do something fast or they were going to die."

Incredibly Lorenzo somehow made his way through the deadly smoke and flames in a blink of an eye and found the fallen firemen. "I could see one of my friends pinned under the wall and the side of his face was burning while I stood there," says Lorenzo. "I knew I had to get that wall off of them, and I didn't have any time to get help. It was up to me." Lorenzo had to act fast. He reached down into the flames without any protection and grabbed the wall with his own bare hands. Then he somehow summoned the strength to lift the 1,000-pound wall into the air and off of his friends. "Still to this day, I don't know what gave me the strength to do that," says Lorenzo. "The most I ever lifted before in my life was 400 pounds. All I know is that I couldn't let them die. I had to help the friends I loved." Despite smoke pouring into his lungs and flames scalding his unprotected body, Lorenzo held up the mammoth wall with one hand while he pulled two firemen out with the other hand. Three more men scrambled on their own to safety. Then he dropped the wall and hurried from the deadly flames himself.

The two men Lorenzo yanked from the fire were rushed to the hospital and survived thanks to Lorenzo's inexplicable feat. None of his friends could explain how he did it. But they didn't care. They only knew he had saved their lives, and they would be indebted to him for the rest of their lives.

Lorenzo was awarded for his bravery by the state of California. "Just seeing them alive was reward enough," says Lorenzo. "But the medal was nice." The tale of Lorenzo's amazing life was far from over though. Soon after his heroic act, he received an even greater award, a Rottweiler puppy from one of the firefighters he'd pulled from the flames. Of all the gifts he could have given Lorenzo, none could have been sweeter. After losing his beloved dog as a child, being given one for being a hero was like a validation of his whole life. "It really gave me back my heart," says Lorenzo. "I knew I was doing the right thing with my life."

Lorenzo aptly named the dog Cinder because of the fire that brought her his way and the two bonded fast. They did everything together and Cinder was always by her master's side. At the end of the day the dutiful dog grew accustomed to falling asleep on her owner's chest listening to the gentle beat of his heart. The fit fireman liked relaxing on the weekends by taking long hard hikes in the nearby mountains and he made sure he took Cinder along, too.

It was on one of those hikes that Cinder did what she had never done before—she refused to head up the trail. "She just stopped dead in her tracks and wouldn't budge," explains Lorenzo. "I tried talking to her and nudging her, I tried everything, but she wouldn't move an inch. She just sat there as if she was afraid of the same old hill she'd been up a hundred times before." Thinking that Cinder might be sick, thoughtful Lorenzo immediately returned home intent on calling the vet for his beloved pooch.

But upon their return home, Lorenzo felt his chest tighten and sharp pains shoot through his body. Then he collapsed on the floor. "I knew my heart had given out," says Lorenzo. "As a fireman I knew the signs all too well. And I knew I would die if I didn't get help." Alone and unable to lift himself up to get to a phone and too weak to even scream for help, Lorenzo laid helplessly on the floor while his loving dog looked on in sympathetic horror. Then the dog did something Lorenzo never expected and will never forget.

As the noble fireman prayed for help, Cinder suddenly ran to the other end of the room and jumped up several feet onto the kitchen counter, grabbed the phone between her teeth and brought it to her master's side. "For a second I thought maybe I had passed out and I was dreaming this or something," reveals Lorenzo. "But when I felt the phone in my hand and Cinder by my side I knew it was real." Lorenzo quickly dialed 911 and told them he was in cardiac arrest. Within minutes the lifesaving paramedics along with Lorenzo's fire and rescue friends were there to save him. They stabilized him and then rushed him to the hospital where he was nursed back to health.

"She saved my life," says Lorenzo. "There's not a doubt in my mind that I would have been dead if it wasn't for her." Doctors confirmed that Cinder's actions had indeed saved Lorenzo. Cinder was named dog hero of the year by the Los Angeles SPCA (Society for Prevention of Cruelty to Animals) for her bravery. Since then the two heroes have grown closer than ever.

But most important, Lorenzo knows that Cinder saving his life was just one more chapter of a lifetime of love's rewards. "So many people were there to save me along the way," says Lorenzo. "That's why I was there to save those men, and why Cinder was here to save me. We all need each other in this world. And that's what being a hero is really about."

Frozen Hearts of Love

~ ~ ~

*C*ilia and George were in love once upon a time. And that's when they were blessed with two girls, Rayann and Sheela. They started their hugely successful real estate company on the outskirts of Denver, Colorado, and achieved just about everything they wanted in life with each other's help and love.

But then somewhere along the line something went wrong, and suddenly everything they loved about each other became the very things they despised. Still in high school when they met, Cilia at first loved the way George protected her and took control of every situation. But as she grew into a woman and a professional she resented how he always wanted to have the final say on things. "I felt smothered by him and unable to grow as a woman," remembers Cilia. "It was as if I was living with my father, and I just wanted to escape." Meanwhile George didn't know what to think and how to act around his wife anymore. Though he always listened to her ideas and loved how opinionated she was, he was accustomed to making the ultimate decision when push came to shove, and he always felt she wanted that from him. "She was like two different people trapped in one, and I didn't know which one wanted what from me," remembers George. They tried their best to make things work, but eventually they both threw in the towel, figuring the situation was hopeless.

The once-happy couple divorced in 1981 after fifteen years together. Their children who were both in high school at the time were devastated. Though no longer committed to their marriage, the parents were devoted to their children, and they wanted to do everything they could to protect them through the terrible ordeal. So they worked out a deal to do just that. "We figured we had always made good decisions together about the children's upbringing," says George. "So why not at least try to continue to raise them together. We thought that way it might be easier on them."

George and Cilia were also very committed to their joint business and decided to continue to run that together as well. So even after George moved out of the house, the couple still saw each other every day at the office and talked almost every other night about their daughters. They both began seeing other people shortly after the divorce was final but never very seriously. And this is how life went on for the couple for almost a year.

But then their friendship began going south over work issues. At first they were just disagreeing, but before long they were bickering almost as much as when they were married. "We were having the exact same arguments we had when we were living together," admits Cilia. "No matter what we did we couldn't get along for even a few hours together at the office. We had never had problems at the office before. At home yes, but never at work." Everything became difficult. Every aspect of their communication slowly eroded until finally they were ready to sell their company and distance themselves completely from each other.

But worse still, they were starting to fight over the children as well—a topic they had never argued about before. They fought over what college their girls should attend, when the girls should have their curfew, who they could date. Whatever George wanted to do, Cilia rejected and visa versa. It was an all-out war, and the girls were in the middle. "We always made it a point to be a single voice when it came to the children," says George. "Now we were as divided as possible, and I knew it was affecting our children. But we just couldn't seem to get it together."

As George and Cilia fought, their daughters bore the brunt of the damage. Their teenage girls just wanted their parents to get along, and their war was taking its toll on them emotionally. One day George and Cilia found out the hard way just how much they were hurting their children when they both received a phone call from the local sheriff. Their daughters had been arrested at a nightclub for being underage and intoxicated. Worse still, the oldest daughter, Rayann, was in possession of several grams of cocaine. Both Cilia and George were devastated. It was all too apparent to them that their constant fighting and strife were threatening their children's well-being and their futures. They knew something had to be done to fix their family even if it was just to find a way to be happily divorced.

For the sake of their children, they agreed to work at getting along a little better and to take a class in positive parenting. The class was a weekend seminar at a mountain retreat outside of Denver. So the battling exes set out together one Friday afternoon after leaving the office while their kids stayed with their grandparents for the weekend. It was the first time in a long time that they really knew they were doing the right thing when their daughters thanked them and saw them off with a big hug. Their daughters' unconcealed joy comforted Cilia and George as they headed off to try and patch up their parenting skills.

Traffic was bad on the way out of town, so George decided to take an out-of-the-way back-road route that would get them off the main highway. But what George could never have predicted was the fierce and unexpected winter storm that was descending upon them.

As they drove deeper into the wilderness through treacherous mountain passes, which were already packed with snow, the beautiful backwoods quickly turned dark and dangerous. Within a few hours the wind kicked up, the snow thickened and the winding roads became a sheet of ice. It was impossible to go any farther. "It all happened so fast," remembers George. "All of a sudden we were in the middle of this terrible storm, and all I could do was pull over and wait for it to pass." But as George struggled to see through the snow and find a safe place to pull over, he couldn't see the deadly ten-foot drop that was concealed by the freshly fallen snow. As he edged unknowingly toward the cliff, the car began to slide and then finally, in one swift and horrifying moment, dropped off the road into a gully headfirst. "The first thought that went through my mind was about George," reveals Cilia. "I remember thinking how much I still cared about him. I couldn't believe I was feeling that, but I was."

Remarkably, both George and Cilia were only shaken and bruised by the deadly drop, but the car was demolished. The front windshield as well as the driver's side window were shattered to pieces. And the vehicle was immovable. As the two sat there in the demolished vehicle trying to assess the situation it seemed as if things were about as bad as they could get. But they grew worse. Suddenly they were in the middle of an all-out blizzard. "I couldn't see a foot past the car," remembers George. "The wind was gusting something fierce and the car was filling up with snow." Cilia and George quickly took whatever refuge they could in the backseat of the SUV sticking their luggage up against the front window hoping it would at least deflect some of the snow and the biting, cold wind. But despite their efforts, as night fell so did the temperature, and they knew that this had now become a life-or-death fight for survival. They were in the middle of nowhere and the odds of anyone finding them were slim, especially in such a fierce storm. Their only hope was to survive until sunup when they could walk the forty miles or so back to the main road for help. "It was the first time in our relationship that I was really scared and didn't feel the need to fake being macho with Cilia," admits George. "I just let her know what I was feeling."

Unable to start the stalled engine to generate heat, they were forced to rely on body heat to stay as warm as possible and two bodies were warmer than one. As the former couple huddled together in the backseat for survival, it brought back bittersweet memories. "We used to crawl up in the backseat of my dad's station wagon and get warm in the winter when we were in high school," says Cilia. "I'd forgotten how nice that was. Somehow even in the midst of that tragedy it felt good. But at the same time it hurt

because I realized how much we had messed up our lives."
As the dead of night sent the temperature plunging, they
clung to each other for dear life.

As they became colder and colder the need for sleep
grew more and more difficult to resist. Growing up in Colorado, they both knew that falling asleep in below-zero
temperatures without cover was a sure recipe for death.
They took turns rubbing each other to increase their circulation and to stay awake to fight the numbing cold. They
started singing songs to keep their minds alert. Soon the
melodies took them back to the songs they had sung together when they first got married. The reminiscent tone
and the situation brought tears to Cilia's eyes and she broke
down, apologizing to George. "She kept telling me 'I'm
sorry,' " remembers George. "But I was never mad at her.
She didn't need to apologize. It occurred to me that we
both had been so wrapped up in our own worlds over the
last few years, we hadn't given each other a chance. Now
we had to be sensitive to each other for survival."

When they ran out of song lyrics they both could remember, Cilia had an even better idea. She began reciting
something she never would forget—the original and poetic
wedding vows they had written for each other so many
years ago. "To this noble man before me," started Cilia, "I
am honored to promise all that I am and ever will be to
you. And I will never put my needs before yours nor neglect or abandon you in time of need or hardship. I will

love you forever whether old or young, sick or well, rich or poor. I will cherish you and respect you even when the rest of the world turns its back. For you are me and I am you and without each other we have only half a life." She continued the vows in their entirety. And when she finished George felt the rush of love and warmth he felt the day he married Cilia. "I forgot about the cold," reveals George. "I felt so good inside. I'll never forget those words or the ones I told her." The moment Cilia was done reciting her vows, he recited his. "I love you and I promise to always love you in every way I can and with every ounce of my strength," declared George. "I will give you everything that is mine so that all I have is ours. And I will fight to be your man and your defender, your lover and your friend for as long as blood flows through my veins. For without you I am without purpose in this world."

The strong words lit bonfires in their souls that no cold could temper. They were in love, and they always had been. Now they realized just how much they needed each other. "As I evolved from a high school girl into a successful business woman I guess I felt I was changing," explains Cilia. "And I didn't think that I could grow with him. But I realized as I clung to him there that I couldn't grow without him. With him I could do anything. I just had to be honest about what I needed." George finally realized he just needed to be patient with the love of his life. "I was ready to give her whatever she needed—time, space—whatever," reveals George. "I just prayed we'd make it out of this so I could give her all that." As George and Cilia repeated their vows to each other over and over again the night passed, and before they knew it the warm sun was rising. When daylight broke George and Cilia were still alive.

The next morning as Denver papers reported the heavy winter storm that cut power to thousands and left roads impassable all over the state, the snow stopped falling. The newly inspired lovebirds shared a long and deep kiss before George emerged from the SUV ready to make the long trek back to civilization on foot. As he prepared to go it alone, Cilia rose to her feet and took his hand to accompany him down that long road. "I wasn't letting him go ever again," says Cilia, "not then, not ever. We're in this life together—for keeps."

Putting Stock in Love

*H*arvey started his Internet company from the ground up. His brainchild was a business that helped small local retailers sell merchandise over the Web. His innovative techniques won him great praise and lots of accounts, and his company grew by leaps and bounds in the first two years. "I was doing what I always dreamed about—owning my own shop, and I was creating a lot of jobs and making my employees happy while living a great life at the same time. Life was good," says Harvey.

But five years later, the forty-five-year-old husband and father of two sons was still working twelve-hour days six days a week to make his dream work. He was so exhausted by the time he got home from work that he didn't have the time nor energy to enjoy his prosperity with his family. "I still loved my company, but it was too hard to keep working like that," explains Harvey. "I wanted the opportunity to spend time at home." Harvey decided to take the company public and use the money to grow the upper management team and infrastructure so that he could pay more attention to his family while other competent executives ran the place.

To get started, Harvey hired a big-time financial analyst to appraise the company's worth and establish how he could raise the offering price as high as possible. Harvey expected the analyst to advise him on how to best present the company's image to the buying public, but he immediately began telling him how to run his company. "He had all these ideas for how to quickly increase the profit margin of the company with cost-cutting measures," says Harvey. That's not really what I wanted. I knew I ran my company well. But I wasn't opposed to listening to what he had to say."

As the numbers man worked diligently on pumping up the profits in an effort to boost the offering price, he came up with a great idea to save money—fire a third of the staff. The analyst explained how Harvey could cut his entire middle-management team during the transition of the company and almost double the profits. Then after the offering, his new upper-management team would handle all the responsibilities of the people he fired and then some. But in the meantime, before hiring those executives, the profit margin would soar because of the tremendous decrease in salary output and the company wouldn't suffer the loss of management because during that short period Harvey could make all management decisions as he had done years before.

In truth, Harvey knew that many of those middle managers would have to be let go in the long run anyway because of the restructuring of the company. But he was planning on giving them notice and buying out their contracts with money from the offering, thereby securing their financial safety. But he felt that letting them go like this was just too harsh, although it could raise the price of the offering and bring millions of additional dollars. "It all sounded great except for one thing—the people's lives I was going to ruin," says Harvey. "What about them?" Harvey needed time to think. He took a month off and spent it with his family.

Meanwhile, it didn't take long for rumors of a personnel shakeup to spread through his company. "Everybody down there knew I was going public," remembers Harvey. "And they knew this analyst was trying to cut costs. So I was fielding a slew of phone calls at home from my managers asking me what was happening." Suddenly people were afraid they were going to lose their jobs, so Harvey needed to make a decision fast.

But what Harvey never expected was that his loyal team of middle managers, who were unaware that it was actually their jobs that were on the line, would sacrifice their own livelihoods for the rest of the employees. They came over to his house and pitched an idea he'll never forget. "They assumed I was thinking about cutting out some of the lower rung of employees," explains Harvey. "So they told me not to do it because those people couldn't afford to lose the money. They actually offered to take a cut in their own salaries so we could keep those people onboard. They agreed to take a ten percent pay cut for the sake of the others." Harvey was astounded. Here they were giving up their salaries to help others, when they didn't even realize it was their jobs on the line. Harvey was totally overcome with their generosity. He told them he'd consider their offer.

Now Harvey was in a state of serious confusion. How on earth could he lay those managers off—any of them? But there was still the money. And it was Harvey's company and his livelihood in question. "I'm a businessman," says Harvey. "And I know I have to look very carefully at all my alternatives for increasing profits. After all, I run a business and its purpose is to make money. I work very hard for that."

As Harvey pondered the difficult decision before him, someone very close to him helped him make his mind up. That special someone was his seven-year-old son, Steven. One day, while playing cards with Steven for Tootsie Rolls, Harvey was down pretty low and getting ready to concede victory when Steven surprised him by suddenly handing over half his chips à la Tootsie Rolls to his dad. "As he was handing me his chips, I told him he didn't have to do that. Then he says, 'Mom told me whenever you give something away you get back twice as much.' Well he must have thought I was sick or something, because I just fell back in my chair in shock." The words stung Harvey's heart. The next day he announced his plans to go public and give all his management team a five percent raise so they could work that much harder during the transition.

The company greatly outperformed expectations on "The Street" and Harvey is now happily running his multimillion dollar company from the beaches of Aruba, confident that his loyal team of middle managers are outperforming their expectations!

"It's true that in business sometimes to win you have to act like you are in a rat race," says Harvey. "But I'm also a member of the human race and winning that race is a lot more important to me."

Prisoners of Love

Nine-year-old Mary should have been terrified when Japanese troops armed with rifles and bayonets stormed her British boarding school in Northeast China at the height of World War II. But the daughter of English missionaries, who had been separated from her parents by the war, wasn't afraid because of the courageous support and protection of her loving teachers. They risked their lives to keep up the children's spirits and convince them that they were in no danger.

"Those women were real heroes," says Mary of her boarding school teachers. "As we were marched into the prison camp, they made us sing our religious hymns and acted as if we were just on a field trip or something. They made us feel safe and secure." Even as Japanese soldiers marked them as property of the Emperor of Japan, Mary's teachers stood up and insisted they be allowed to continue to teach their students, holding classes every day within the concentration camp using fruit crates for chairs and desks. Refusing to allow the children to be affected by the indignities of war, they gave the students self-respect and instilled character in a situation where survival was a blessing. For three long years, those teachers made sure the children learned, grew and felt safe and secure. "They used to tell us we were prisoners on the outside but not on the inside," remembers Mary. "They were in the business of keeping up the spirit, and that was our inspiration."

The loving teachers helped the students deal with rancid food, unbearable cold and incarceration while still maintaining their sense of dignity and grace. " 'God didn't make one set of rules for the Princess of Buckingham Palace and another set for you,' they used to tell us," remembers Mary. "Here we were eating out of tin cans and soap dishes, but they refused to let us act like animals. They never let us give up hope or lose our spirit. They knew the most important thing children need to feel is a sense of normalcy and knowing what to expect everyday. They made sure we had that no matter what." Knowing that children needed order and structure to feel safe, every day the courageous teachers and protectors risked their lives to stand up to their Japanese captors and insist that the children say their prayers, do their lessons, and keep up their spirits. They argued for sports equipment and games for the children, all the time never letting the children know that they were ever in jeopardy. "I didn't realize that we were even in any danger," reveals Mary. "For instance I only learned years later that people actually were shot at the camp. We felt that if we obeyed our teachers just as we did before, everything was going to be alright. We saw the guard dogs and the armed guards, but the teachers made us feel so secure it didn't bother us."

But while young Mary was completely insulated from fear, her parents were out of their minds with worry in unoccupied China trying to find out what became of their daughter. When they learned that she was in a Japanese concentration camp, they immediately feared the worst, terrified by horrific tales of the rapes, murders and atrocities committed by Japanese soldiers as they invaded and conquered their way across China. "I didn't know it then, but my mother was crying herself to sleep every night just thinking about what could be happening to me," says Mary.

Meanwhile Mary's teachers kept the children happy and hopeful while they prayed for the day when they were finally liberated from their captors. Their prayers were finally answered on August 17, 1945. "It was a beastly hot day," remembers Mary. "And out of nowhere we saw angels dropping from the sky to save us." Unbeknownst to the camp, Japan had surrendered, the war was over, and the angels were American soldiers parachuting into the camp to free them once and for all. Wild cheering and hoorays broke out as children and adults all swarmed the men who came to free them.

Mary was reunited with her parents several weeks later. And after gorging herself on the waffles and ice cream her mother had prepared especially for her, Mary and her mother hugged and cried, thankful to be alive and together again.

After the war her parents moved to the United States and started a farm in Michigan and Mary thought the worst was over. But when she was fourteen years old, life became tough again when the carefree teen was playing with a friend and got her hand caught in a buzz saw, ripping it from her arm. The hand was later reattached but with limited mobility. Now her father came to her rescue ready to love, support, and inspire her to fight for a fulfilling and meaningful life despite her infirmity. "This is a whole other beautiful story of how my father just poured hope into my soul," says Mary proudly. "My daddy believed in me. He told me handicaps have nothing to do with the inside. He said his 'Mary Sweetheart had no handicaps on the inside.' "

Mary learned to live with her handicap and obtained her college degree in journalism before going on to become a high school English teacher in a troubled inner-city school in Camden, New Jersey. "I believed in my students and what they could achieve," says Mary. "And I used the principles of compassion that I learned from my father and the elements of structure and discipline which made me feel safe in the camp to inspire them to overcome their surroundings." Frequently allowing students who needed extra help to form study groups at her own home, she prided herself on empowering the students to beat the odds against them in the crime-ridden community.

In fact, Mary made such an important impression on her students that almost twenty years later one of them grew up to become an elected state official in New Jersey. He called on the retired teacher to put the lessons of her days in the concentration camp to work for troubled youths as the director of a detention facility for minors awaiting trial on charges ranging from robbery and assault to drug trafficking and murder. The problem center was described by newspapers all over the state as unfit for animals and was infamous for its harsh conditions and frequent rioting. "I was now a homemaker and this was the last thing I ever could have seen myself doing," says Mary. "But the more I thought about it the more it made sense if I could help these kids with the same principles that kept me alive and well in the concentration camp."

Mary took the job and her skills were put to the test the first week. While sitting down to enjoy a dinner party with friends one night, she received a startling phone call from the center and learned that a riot had broken out. Inmates and guards were wounded and had squared off against each other in a dangerous stalemate.

Still in her evening gown, Mary, the compassionate warden, rushed to the rescue. "None of the guards thought there was any way I'd be able to handle this, but I walked right in there unafraid and just talked to the children and made them feel safe and secure," remembers Mary. "These were children behind bars just like I was in the camp. They longed for normalcy in a very abnormal situation. They wanted to hear about my dinner party, so I told them all about it." Mary also assured the youths that from now on they would be as vigorously rewarded for good behavior as they were punished for disruptive behavior using the tender ways of her father to help comfort the traumatized youths.

Mary then proceeded to use the shining example of how her World War II protectors inspired her during the war to help these children. Despite the fact that they were behind bars, she made daily schooling the number one priority and made sure the children were really learning. And then she instituted activities to occupy their minds and enrich their hearts, such as an official newspaper written and illustrated by the inmates themselves. "With the newspaper, I tell them that they are important and what they have to say is important," says Mary. "Plus, writing for the paper gives them a meaningful routine that they can depend on being part of their lives. Again that adds to that feeling of order and safety."

With Mary's honest and hardworking efforts the program garnered national recognition for its success. But the real success in Mary's eyes is the feeling of trust and security the students have begun to experience which enables them to heal and potentially rectify their lives. "We have kids who jump entire grade levels while they are in here," says Mary. "And I am so encouraged when I read the letters from former inmates who have changed their lives." It's those success stories that make Mary feel like she's making miracles possible, like the story of a young man accused of second degree murder who Mary helped to get his life back together and who just recently sent her his college graduation announcement for receiving his engineering degree from one of America's premier universities. Or the teenage hard-hearted career-criminal wannabe who was transformed so dramatically by Mary's compassion and discipline that after several months in the center he looked up at her with tears in his eyes and told her he wished she was his mom.

"That's why I come here every day, and that's why I will never stop fighting to save these children," says Mary. Instilling a sense of safety, order and meaning to their lives while caring about their hearts, Mary continues to make a difference by standing up for the rights of minors in criminal cases throughout the justice system. And it's all because someone cared to do the same for her so many years ago. Those are lessons she'll never forget.

"One person can make a difference in the life of a child,"

says Mary. "The lessons I learned under fire are the same lessons I'm trying to teach children today who are under fire. The message of hope kept us alive in the camps and it will keep these kids alive too if they'll hear it."

Someone to Help

*L*ife wasn't supposed to be like this for little girls, thought Jody. Her father wasn't supposed to decide he didn't want her before she was born. And her mother wasn't supposed to abandon her when she was four years old along with her one-year-old brother, Josh, and her newborn sister, Tabatha. Most of all, she wasn't supposed to look into a mirror one day when she was seven years old to see the whites of her eyes yellow because she was dying of liver failure. More than ever, Jody needed someone to love her—*someone to help.* "I didn't understand why all these bad things were happening to me, and I was scared," reveals Jody. "If it wasn't for my grandparents there to protect me I know I never would have pulled through."

Growing up on the outskirts of Fort Worth, Texas, her aging grandparents were her only salvation when her mother flew the coop in 1981, leaving her and her siblings parentless. After countless tests and a month in the hospital, doctors told poor Jody that her liver was failing and she needed a transplant. But her caring grandparents refused to tell her the whole awful truth—that she was going to die unless she got that transplant. "They shielded me from so much of the scary stuff," says Jody. "They told me I was sick and that I needed an operation, but they never said the 'D' word. I don't think I could have handled it if I knew how sick I really was."

While administrators searched for a donor liver, doctors sent Jody home from the hospital with her grandparents to their tiny ramshackle house, where Jody and her makeshift family of five scraped to get by on her retired grandparents' meager pension. But when they learned that even if they could find a liver for their granddaughter the lifesaving surgery would cost $125,000. It was as good as a death sentence for little Jody. Once again Jody needed *someone to help*.

As her grandparents agonized over what to do in their darkest hour, the answer came in an unexpected knock on the door one day from a man who wanted to help. A local Shriner and oil salesman had heard Jody's sad story from his wife, the nurse at Jody's school. He told her grandparents that he was going to get the whole town to chip in to pay for the transplant. "I remember my grandmother crying when he told her," says Jody. "She said it was the answer to her prayers. I still didn't know how important it was. But I thanked him anyway. Little did I know that he was saving my life." A few days later Jody's health took a turn for the worse, and the suffering child was forced back into the hospital where doctors battled to keep her alive while they continued to search for a liver.

Meanwhile, the helpful gentleman stayed true to his word to help Jody raise the money she needed to survive, and indeed he set out to get the job done. But now HE needed *someone to help* HIM. He convinced the entire town to come to the rescue. The 5,000 inhabitants coughed up all their pennies, nickels, dimes, and quarters into milk jars at checkout stands all over town. They held a special town auction where caring citizens sold off unwanted items and donated the proceeds to the ailing little girl. They even held a runners' race to raise money. The sensitive salesman also talked the county commissioners into donating $10,000 to the Save Jody Fund.

As Jody sat in her hospital bed her grandparents gave her uplifting updates on how the town was going to bat for her. And it felt good being cared for. "It was as if everyone in that town was my friend all of a sudden," says Jody. "People I didn't even know wanted to help me. After you've been abandoned by your own mother, I can't tell you how good it feels to know that you're not alone in the world—

that people really do care about you." The people poured out their hearts and their money to help Jody. But it still wasn't enough for the expensive procedure. Now THE TOWN needed somebody outside to pitch in, they needed *someone to help*. Finally the Children's Medical Center in Dallas where Jody would receive her transplant heard about the incredible effort to assist the young girl and was compelled to kick in a whopping $15,000 to give the little girl a life.

When Jody heard the good news she couldn't have been happier, that is unless they told her they actually had a liver for her, but they didn't and now the tough little fighter had to hang on until they did. But she couldn't do it alone. Again, she needed *someone to help*.

Her grandparents answered the call as best as they could, comforting her and keeping her company throughout the long days of waiting, then sleeping every night in her hospital room with her. "I remember her grandfather just sitting there in a rocking chair all day with her," says one of the hospital staff. "Sometimes Jody would climb up on his lap and he'd hold her for hours." They brought her in her favorite foods and carted in friends from school to lift her spirits. Her brother and sister were there to lend their moral support too and tell her how important she was to them. But her family couldn't keep her spirits up alone, they all needed *someone to help*.

This time it was the nurses in Children's Hospital who

went the extra mile to come to her aid. "They were like my best friends when I was in there," remembers Jody. "They went out of their way to make me feel like a normal kid. They made me forget about the pain and the fear of what was going to happen. They made me have fun." The nurses certainly did their job when it came to Jody. Yes, they first fulfilled all their medical duties by doing all the things that nurses do. But these nurses went far beyond their duty to help Jody. When they found out Jody liked animals, the nurses convinced the hospital to allow them to take Jody on their days off to the zoo for a well-needed reprieve from the cold and sterile hospital home she had been confined to for two months. "The koala bears were my favorite," remembers Jody. "They were so happy and carefree." Then another nurse decided to take Jody shopping for clothes on her day off. "That made me feel like a little girl again," says Jody. "I hadn't been able to do those girl things for so long." And the rest of the nurses practically camped out in Jody's room playing games and telling her jokes—anything to take her mind off of the pain and the predicament she was in. "They were my heroes," says Jody, "and I decided then that I wanted to grow up and be just like them. I wanted to be a nurse and help children."

One February day Jody overcame the greatest of odds with the help of her grandparents, her brother and sister, a selfless salesman and his nurse wife, an entire town and a hospital full of feeling nurses and administrators determined to save her, not to mention countless friends and supporters all over the county. She received a brand-new healthy, lifesaving liver. "I still didn't understand that I could die without the transplant," says Jody. "But just by the way everyone was looking at me when they told me I was getting the liver I could tell there was something very important about what was happening. Most of all I was looking forward to not hurting anymore and getting out of the hospital."

The operation was a success but for the next year Jody battled on-and-off-again rejection of her new liver. In and out of the hospital, she again depended upon the same cast of characters for support, namely her grandparents. So when her grandfather passed away while she was back in the hospital it was a devastating blow. "By this time, I understood that I was fighting for my life," says Jody. "And so when my grandfather died in the middle of me being so sick with the rejection it was hard to take. I missed him so much. Most of all I was heartbroken for my grandma." Stuck in the hospital by herself while her grandfather was buried Jody again needed *someone to help*.

As she sat crying alone in her room, one of her favorite nurses walked in and told her to hop out of bed and get ready, she was taking her to her grandfather's funeral. "That really meant a lot to me," says Jody. "I loved him so much and I needed to say goodbye."

Jody made it through the rejection period to a clean bill

of health. But incredibly, the hardships she'd face were far from over. A year later her twelve-year-old brother Josh died in a freak accident when he drowned after slipping into a flash flood wash. Soon after that, one of the girls whom she had met in the hospital and developed a strong friendship with died after failing to get a transplant. And at a time when Jody needed more than ever the stability and support of family, Jody lost her only guardian when her grandmother began suffering the effects of Alzheimer's disease and needed to move to a nursing home. "It was all happening at once," says Jody. "I didn't understand why these bad things had to happen. But I knew I just had to keep going so I could keep my promise to become a nurse and help people." No longer a little girl, the blossoming young woman was hurting inside, and more important she was all alone. Again Jody more than ever needed *someone to help*.

When her older, second-cousin Carol heard what happened, she asked without hesitation Jody and her sister to come live with her and her husband, John. It was all Jody could have hoped for. Now she had a family and a home once again. She was safe and secure. Within a few short months she grew to love her kind and considerate cousins like the parents she never truly had. And for the first time in her life, Jody had a mom and dad better than any child could ever wish for.

Jody went on to achieve great happiness and success in

high school, belonging to the National Honor Society, band council, and the yearbook staff. But most important, she worked toward keeping her promise to become a nurse and help others when she graduated. In her senior year she applied to Texas Women's University to study nursing, but it wasn't going to be easy. Despite the fact that she worked thirty hours a week through high school, money was lean and college was expensive. But little did Jody know that out there still was *someone to help*.

As Jody proudly walked down the aisle at her high school graduation a surprise announcement filled the air. The town's education foundation was donating $16,000 to help Jody with college. "I thought I was hearing things," says Jody. "It was the happiest day of my life. But not because they were giving me the money—because they were helping me to achieve my dream of helping others."

Jody put the money to good use, working diligently through college. When things got tough in school because money was tight, once again there was *someone to help*—the same nurses who took care of her years before in the hospital. They bought her textbooks and nursing supplies.

With their help and so many others, Jody successfully graduated and became a registered nurse. And she immediately applied and was hired to work with heart and kidney transplant patients at Children's Medical Center in Dallas, Texas,—the very same hospital where she was given the gift of life.

Nowadays, as one of the longest-living recipients of a liver transplant, Jody reminds herself everyday of the many people that made that possible. And that makes it easy for her to remember that now it's her turn to be that special someone when a child needs *someone to help*.

Love Connections

The worst was already over for many in Dayton, Ohio, as they faced the aftermath of one of the deadliest string of tornadoes to hit the United States on April 4, 1974. During a sixteen-hour period 148 separate twisters touched down across the bread basket of the country, leaving in their wake 315 dead and thousands more injured.

But as twelve-year-old Tina rose from the rubble of a stranger's house where she had taken refuge, all she wanted to do was find her ten-year-old brother, Aiden. "I was covered in blood, but I didn't even realize it because I was so worried about my brother," says Tina. "I had to find him!"

Tina and Aiden had gotten caught up in the tornado while on their way back home from the mall. They stopped to play baseball at a local park with some other kids and Tina lost track of time and her brother. "I don't know what I was thinking just letting him wander off like that, but I was stupid, and I paid for that mistake," says Tina.

At approximately 4:00 P.M., the sky suddenly grew dark and an ominous funnel cloud appeared in the sky. Petrified parents in the park scrambled to get their children to safety. Tina hurried to find her brother, but he was nowhere in sight. "I got crazy when I couldn't find him," says Tina. "I wasn't going to leave that park without him." And with the park almost deserted a concerned parent grabbed Tina and insisted she come with her back to her house across the street to weather the storm. Tina refused at first but finally gave in to the offer of shelter. "I couldn't stop crying," says Tina. "I was so scared that he was going to die. I didn't want to go, but she refused to leave me out there alone." The helpful single mom and her two children prepared for the storm back at her house with Tina in tow, but the fast approaching storm didn't give them much time. They huddled together for dear life in the bathroom, waiting for the worst.

Then, in an instant, it hit. "It sounded like the whole world was blowing up," remembers Tina. "I was as scared as I've ever been in my life." The terrible twister ripped off the roof of the tiny house and leveled the walls in one fell swoop. Within seconds it was gone just as fast as it came. Amazingly, Tina and her new friends survived with only cuts and bruises. Tina was hurt the worst from a piece of flying glass which badly cut her face. But none of that mattered now because she was determined to find her little brother.

Bleeding, Tina ran out of the house as the helpful stranger screamed for her to come back. "The only thing I cared about then was finding Aiden," recalls Tina. "If anything happened to him I couldn't live with myself." Tina ran frantically through the unfamiliar streets around the ballpark where she had last seen her brother. The destruction was horrible. It reminded the young girl of all the pictures she'd seen in school books of wars in far-off lands. While Tina scrambled to locate Aiden, her streaming tears and the blood from her cuts ran together on her face to form a ghastly rouge. Tina pressed a rag against the wounds to try and stop the bleeding. From one demolished house to the next she wandered frantically back and forth until she canvassed the area, but her brother was nowhere. "I was running out of ideas," says Tina. "And everybody else was dealing with their own tragedies. It seemed like there were dead people everywhere. It was so horrible. But I wasn't going home until I found my brother." Everytime Tina came to a house where tragedy had touched down it terrified her that much more that the same fate had met her little brother. After three hours of fruitless searching she still refused to give up or go home until she found him.

Then, as night fell, she wandered back to the baseball

park to check the area again. That's when she heard a faint cry coming from a pile of rubble that used to be a field keeper's maintenance house. Almost in disbelief, she headed for the demolished house. As she drew closer, she was sure she recognized the cries of her little brother, Aiden, and she spied a faint glimpse of what looked like her brother's red Cincinnati Reds jacket. Tina ran toward the rubble and as she arrived she discovered her brother lying beneath the remnants of the house—his eyes shut and his body mangled and bloody. Terrified, she felt for a pulse as she had learned to do in the CPR class she had taken at the community swimming pool last summer. He was alive! "I was so grateful I remember screaming, 'Thank You God,' over and over again," reveals Tina. "But now I knew I had to get him help pretty fast or he might not make it. I could tell he was hurt bad."

Tina left her brother and ran for help. A block away she spotted a fire and rescue truck and frantically waved them down. They immediately radioed for assistance and a few minutes later Tina and the rescue squad were rushing her brother to the hospital. "I held his hand and prayed the whole way there," says Tina. "I wasn't going to let him die." As they arrived at the hospital, Aiden suddenly regained consciousness and screamed in pain. They rushed him into the ER and doctors determined Aiden was bleeding internally with broken bones from head to foot.

Meanwhile, police tracked down the children's mother

and father, who were uninjured. Tina and Aiden's parents rushed to the hospital to care for their children. Doctors performed emergency surgery on Aiden to stop the internal hemorrhaging and relieve pressure on his lungs from several broken ribs. The operation was a success and six hours later Aiden was awake and recovering. Two weeks passed before Aiden left the hospital, and it wasn't long before Tina and her family put back together the pieces of their lives. Their house had been spared the brunt of the storm and insurance took care of the minimal damage.

Four years later, the mighty storm was just a memory, but the bond between Tina and her little brother had grown stronger than ever. "After the tornado we really got close," remembers Tina. "It was like we were more connected and we could read each other's mind all of a sudden." Tina and Aiden did everything together from riding their bikes back and forth to school every day to hanging out on weekends at the popular local games arcade to wasting the summer away at the community pool. "I told him about all the boys I liked and when I had my first kiss," remembers Tina. "I trusted him more than anybody." They were best friends and they shared all their deepest secrets.

Then three days before Tina's sixteenth birthday, the two teens were headed home from school on their bikes when Tina spotted a boy she had had a crush on for years. His name was Brian and he had graduated her high school the year before. Now the 19-year-old knockaround was working part-time as a construction worker and racing around town in his Camaro. He first caught Tina's eye when she was a freshman and he was a junior. "I knew in my heart he was probably trouble when I first met him," admits Tina. "But he was older and I thought that was cool. Plus he had a car. Unfortunately, it doesn't take much more than that to get a girl's interest when she's sixteen." Aiden knew all about her crush on Brian, but he didn't approve. "He really looked out for me," recalls Tina. "Whenever I talked about boys he got really protective."

But Tina usually gave her brother nothing real to worry about. A model, straight-A student, the wholesome blond teenager was class secretary, a championship track runner and the last person anybody ever suspected of getting into trouble. "I was what they used to call squeaky clean," reveals Tina. "If there was a prize for innocence I won it." But when Tina asked her brother to walk her bike home while she went off with Brian in his car, he was very worried.

Aiden insisted Tina come home with him. But when she refused, there wasn't much her younger brother could do. So he reluctantly agreed to her plan, and off she went. But when she wasn't home for dinner that night, Aiden started to worry. "I was really feeling guilty for letting her go off with him like that," says Aiden. And when she still didn't return later in the night, her entire family became frantic.

At ten o'clock that night, her parents contacted the local

police who tried to track Brian down. But the wayward teen was nowhere to be found, and interviews with his friends and family—including his mother—were fruitless. One sleepless night later, the family was in a state of terror. "My parents were trying to act strong for me," says Aiden. "They kept telling me that the police would find her. But I knew she was in trouble. I could feel it. And I wasn't going to wait around for something bad to happen. She didn't let me die in that tornado, and I wasn't going to let her die now."

The next day was Saturday and as noon approached, the police and the neighborhood parents formed a huge task force to search for the missing girl. That's when Aiden headed out on his bike alone despite his parents' and police warnings that he stay at home. "They were concerned that she was in a lot of danger and that I could be endangering myself as well," says Aiden. "But I wasn't giving up on my sister." Five hours later, after checking out every hangout and hole-in-the wall in the neighborhood, he returned to his worried parents without a trace of his sister and even more scared than before. By Sunday night there was still no sign of Tina or Brian.

Desperate to find Tina, Aiden rose early Monday morning so he could get to the schoolyard by six A.M. He convinced his teachers to allow him to spend the entire day going from class to class asking students for any information at all about his missing sister or the whereabouts of the mysterious Brian. About halfway through the day, a young girl came forward and told him something she didn't think was very important. Brian had a favorite hangout which was an abandoned warehouse where he used to take girls he liked. "She never told the police about it because she thought she would get in trouble with her parents since she'd been there with Brian before to make out," explains Aiden. "But when she heard me begging in front of the class it made an impact on her to tell me about it."

Aiden immediately called his parents with the information and they contacted the police. Meanwhile, Aiden decided to check out the out-of-the way warehouse himself. He didn't realize he'd arrive there well before the police did. "I figured they'd be rushing over there with sirens blaring," says Aiden. "But what I found out later was that it doesn't happen like that in real life. They need to check out information and get the proper warrants and all that unless they know for sure that the information is correct and a ten-year-old boy's information is not always so highly regarded." While police were attempting to find the owner of the empty warehouse Aiden started poking around outside of the locked building. "I knew if Brian used to take girls there he either knew the owner and had a key or he used to sneak in somehow," explains Aiden. "So I searched for a way in."

As Aiden tried to get into the building, he also scoured the area looking for any sign of his sister or Brian. That's when he heard what he believed was his sister's voice coming from the back of the building. "It was real hard to hear," says Aiden. "But I knew it was her, I just knew it." Still unable to get into the building, Aiden jumped back on his bike and rushed to find a pay phone and call the police. "I told them I found my sister and she was screaming inside this building," says Aiden. "It was a little bit of a lie because I could barely hear anything, but I knew she was in there, so I took a chance. I figured my sister's life was worth a little fib."

Police rushed to the scene to meet Aiden. But by the time they arrived the faint sounds Aiden heard fell silent. Relying solely on Aiden's account, they broke down the front door and entered in search of Tina. They carefully and cautiously made their way to the back of the building while Aiden waited outside. Seconds later police found Tina beaten and bound with duck tape and left to die. When officers emerged carrying her in their arms Aiden erupted into loud cheers. "I started screaming I was so happy," says Aiden. "I kept screaming her name over and over again. The police actually had to get hold of me and calm me down at one point. I had so much emotion going through me I couldn't control it." Meanwhile, Tina was rushed to the hospital where she was treated for a myriad of traumas and injuries including dehydration.

A few hours later the traumatized teenaged girl was conscious and described to police the grizzly tale of how she had been abducted and raped at gunpoint by Brian then beaten to within inches of her death and left to die. As soon as she was finished giving her statement, she asked to see her brother. "She wanted to talk to me before she saw my parents," says Aiden. "She felt ashamed. I told her it wasn't her fault, but she couldn't stop crying and apologizing."

Three years later, police in Illinois caught Brian when a convenience-store clerk recognized him from a wanted posting and called the authorities. Tina and her brother both testified, enabling prosecutors to secure a guilty verdict which resulted in a twenty-year sentence for Brian.

Tina and Aiden both went on to become physicians. And these days the connection between brother and sister is still as strong as ever as they work together in the same practice. "Family is everything," says Tina. "Without family you really don't have much. But with that love and support anything can happen and just about any tragedy can be overcome."

Man's Best Friend

David hated dogs. As a child he was knocked over in the park by a German shepherd on the Fourth of July and he never got over it. "I know now the dog didn't mean any harm," says David. "But at the time it was terrifying! That dog was as big as a house, and I was so small." Subconsciously, David grew up still fearing that German shepherd and that fear, in time, grew into a hatred of all dogs.

By the time he was thirty-two years old, he was a successful business owner and husband living in the picturesque desert mountains on the outskirts of Phoenix, Arizona. Life was perfect. Until one day when his caring and compassionate wife of three years came home with a Polaroid snapshot of two abandoned dogs she had seen at a local mall as part of a dog-rescue display and wanted to adopt. David was more than just a little displeased—he was downright mad. "Rita knew very well how I felt about dogs," recalls David. "I was really angry that she even was thinking about wanting to bring dogs into the house."

But over the next few days Rita begged her husband to think about adopting the dogs, insisting it would be the best way to get over his fear. "He said that he hated dogs, but I knew in my heart that my husband was a kind and compassionate man who was just suffering from this life-long fear that he had to get over for his own health," reveals Rita. "He would practically break down whimpering every time he even saw a dog." Rita figured this would be a good opportunity to put an end to his phobia. Plus, she genuinely wanted to give these dogs a good home. The two Labrador retrievers Rita wanted to adopt were rescued after being abused by an illegal circus that forced the dogs to perform dangerous and deadly tricks with no regard for their safety. When they refused they were starved and beaten. When they got too old to perform, they were left in the desert to die. On death's door when they were found by the ASPCA, and they desperately needed someone to love them.

Prior to Rita discovering the abused dogs, she and her husband had been trying for the last year and a half to have a child, an effort which had so far been unsuccessful. And they were getting ready to quit trying. "I had a great amount of difficulty getting pregnant," says Rita. "The doctors said again and again nothing was wrong medically, but it wasn't happening. So I kind of used that to talk him into the dogs. If we couldn't have children at least we could have pets."

After countless requests over the next month, David finally gave in to his beloved wife, and they adopted the dogs. "I would do just about anything for my wife," says David, "so even though I hated the idea of getting these dogs, I knew it would make her happy. And I love her too much to deny her being happy. So we became dog owners."

Rita happily took David down to the local shelter where the dogs were waiting and ready for their new family. David tried to pretend he was fine with the whole idea, but his apprehension was apparent. As David met both dogs for the first time, the overjoyed animals stood up on their hind legs and lunged lovingly at David, showing their appreciation by licking his face. But their affection sent David into a frenzy. "He was so obviously petrified," says Rita. "I thought he was going to run away." After filling out all the paperwork, they paid their fees and were told they could pick the dogs up for good the next day. David seemed to appreciate the reprieve.

The next day when they picked up the dogs, David was once again prepared to be scared. But Rita helped to soften the experience as best as she could by holding his hand. The couple took their now-very-happy dogs home and named them Ricky and Lucky. And over the next several months David grew to tolerate his new housemates. Soon he was even liking their company as they became his constant companions. They began each day together with David's morning jog and rarely left his side whenever he was at home. "I couldn't believe how they would just follow him around wherever he would go," says Rita. "They liked him more than me. I must admit I was getting a little jealous, but I was happy to see them helping him to get over his fear." Within a few months, David was as natural with the dogs as if he had loved them his whole life. And so they were soon one big happy family: David, Rita, Ricky and Lucky.

But then the most amazing new development came into their lives—Rita was pregnant. Nine months later Rita gave birth to a beautiful baby girl named Sandy, and the dogs immediately became her protectors. "They were very concerned about making sure she was safe," says Rita. "If she cried they would bark to get my attention. If she was hungry they would know before I did." The dogs' relationship with Sandy grew even closer as she became a toddler. Every night the dogs would cuddle up next to her crib as if to protect her. And when she began to walk, the dogs would escort her, ready to brace her fall should she lose her balance. David was overcome with the love and devotion of the dogs. "If somebody had told me that dogs were capable of that kind of love and support of humans before I wouldn't have believed it," says David. "I was absolutely a dog lover at that point."

But neither David not Rita could ever predict just how far those dogs would go to prove their love for David, Rita, and especially Sandy until one hot summer day when Sandy was three years old. While David was at the store, Rita was at home with Sandy preparing dinner after taking a dip in the pool. The couple had done all they could to make sure their precious little child had no unsupervised access to the pool by erecting a five-foot-tall wrought-iron fortress around it with a solid, heavy iron gate blocking access.

But what they didn't know was on that day the neighbors' kids were playing touch football in their backyard and when the ball flew over the wall and into David and Rita's pool, that fortress would become an open door to disaster. "I guess they didn't want to get in trouble so they didn't bother to come tell me they were going back there to get the ball," says Rita. "They just wandered over the wall and opened the gate and got the ball. But they left the latch open on the way out."

Unaware that any of that had taken place, Rita thought nothing of letting Sandy frolic outside in the backyard with her beloved dogs by her side. Distracted for a moment by the front door bell, Rita took her eyes off of her daughter for a brief minute or two while she went to sign for a package from the mailman. That's when she heard the dogs' wild barks followed by loud splashes. "They were howling as if somebody were killing them," recalls Rita. "So I turned around to look through the back window from where I was. And it looked like the dogs were in the pool dragging something in their mouths. Unable to see Sandy or get a clear view of what the dogs had in their mouths from inside the house, concerned Rita rushed out to the backyard and saw something she will never forget—the devoted dogs had jumped in to save their young damsel in distress after she wandered into the pool, and they were dragging her to safety.

"I thought I was seeing things," says Rita. "Ricky had her collar in his mouth keeping her head above water and Lucky was dragging her toward the shallow end. I immediately jumped in to get my daughter out of there." Rita hoped to dear God Sandy was alive and well as she lifted her limp little body out of the pool. "When I dove in I didn't know what I was going to find," remembers Rita. "I didn't know how long she'd been in." Rita heaved her daughter up on the deck crying, praying, and begging her daughter to talk. Suddenly her little one coughed, then opened her eyes and started to cry. "I hadn't loved hearing her cry that much since the day she was born," reveals Rita. "I knew she was alright."

Rita immediately called the paramedics to make sure her daughter was OK. Sandy was shaken up but alright. However the rescue team confirmed that the dogs had undoubtedly saved her daughter's life. "If she had been under water another minute she may not have survived," says Rita. "And even if she did there probably would have been permanent brain damage."

When David arrived home to find paramedics tending to his daughter he was flabbergasted. And when he heard the story of the protective pooches, he developed a newfound appreciation of them prompting David to change their diet from dog food to well-deserved T-Bones.

Rita and David decided a few months later to fill in their swimming pool and make a nice big and beautiful backyard for Sandy to play in with her canine pals. And David never was scared of another dog ever again. "I decided that this family will always have dogs," says the thankful dad. "They are a part of our family for good. I love them."

Love You Like
a Brother

*B*rothers Mark and Geraldo were inseparable growing up together on the rough streets of the south
side of Chicago. Less than a year apart in age and almost
identical with their big brown eyes and thick locks of black
hair, Mark and Geraldo were such peas in a pod when they
were children that nobody could tell them apart. "We were
always together and we were best friends besides brothers,"
says younger Mark. "I didn't really want to hang out with
any of the other kids in the neighborhood. He was the only
friend I wanted." They played together, ate together,
started school at the same time and learned to ride bikes
with each other.

And they cried together when their parents told them
they were splitting up right after Mark's eighth birthday.

"It was the worst day of our lives," remembers elder sibling Geraldo. "I was so angry, I just wanted to take my brother and run away with him someplace where they couldn't make us cry. We didn't want our dad to leave, but the worst was seeing my brother so sad. I loved him so much and I didn't want him to hurt." The two loving brothers made a promise then that no matter what happened with their parents they would stick by each other through thick and thin.

Their father moved out soon thereafter for a trial separation. Weekend visits with Dad were always tense and too short. But that was just the beginning of their hardships. The separation did nothing to soften their parents' anger toward each other. And they only grew further apart over the next year, making the situation tougher and tougher on the brothers. "Everytime he came to pick us up they would start fighting," remembers Mark. "It was so sad and I would start crying and my brother would start getting real mad. He was always trying to fix the situation to make me happy. But there was nothing that anyone could do." The unrest was tough on both children, but it took the hardest toll on Geraldo. As the oldest, he felt the responsibility to help, and when he couldn't he began taking his anger out on the streets and in the school yard, getting in one fight after another. "I really felt like somehow this was my fault and wanted to be able to make it all better," reveals Geraldo. "I was angry, and I took that anger out on the other kids."

Geraldo quickly spiraled out of control getting in scraps on a daily basis and once even breaking a schoolmate's nose because he asked Geraldo where his father was. As Geraldo became a major discipline problem, his parents' situation only worsened. They bickered and fought their way through pointless talks and hopeless negotiations, which neither of the boys understood before their parents finally decided on a divorce. Though the news came as no surprise to the young boys, what happened next was a total shock. Early one morning the brothers were awakened by their mother and brought down to the courthouse where their parents' divorce was about to be settled by a judge. After sitting through a case neither understood, they were ushered into the judge's chambers where they were told that Geraldo was to move in with his dad while Mark was to stay with his mom.

The boys were devastated. "I remember I couldn't feel my hands or my feet or anything after I heard that," says Geraldo. "It was like I was frozen or something." The two children sat stunned listening to the cruel and unusual ruling. The court had determined that though it was customary in such divorces to award custody to the mother, Geraldo's serious disciplinary problems mandated that he have the strong presence of his father on a daily basis. The cold and impersonal court was trying to break the news compassionately, but it was a hopeless task. "The second I heard those words, I just ran to my brother and clung to him," remembers Mark. "I thought they were going to take him away right then and there, and I was scared. He was my best friend, my only friend. I didn't want him to go." But Geraldo didn't shed a tear. The emotions brewing inside of him were rage and anger. Mostly he was upset with his mother who he blamed for not understanding his father and failing to make him stay. "There are no words for how mad I was," recalls Geraldo. "They had no right to do this. I wanted to just punch somebody."

Less than a month later and two weeks before Christmas, Geraldo was to be picked up by his father and to move across town. But first he decided to let his parents know just how angry he was by getting into some more trouble at school, and this time it was deadly serious. "We were just walking home from school when this kid asked Geraldo if he was being sent away to the crazy hospital," remembers Mark. "That really set him off and he just let into that kid like a maniac." Geraldo picked up a stick on the side of the road and beat the boy senseless. "I thought he was gonna kill him, but thank God the kid was pretty big, otherwise I honestly think he would have," admits Mark.

Later that night the parents of the injured child called the police, and Geraldo was detained on battery charges until his mother and father showed up. He was released pending a hearing, and the next day Geraldo moved away to live with his father. A month later a judge ordered Geraldo to obtain mandatory counseling. The family of the boy opted not to press criminal charges but only asked Geraldo's parents for an apology and to cover their son's medical costs. "Everything was happening so fast and I felt so out of control," remembers Geraldo. "I just wanted to do something to stop all the fighting between my parents. I wanted us to be a happy family again." Geraldo's anger over his parents' split had begun a dangerous disposition for violence that was just the beginning of a long road of crime.

Geraldo and his beloved brother were now at opposite ends of the city and going to different schools, yet at least they were allowed to see each other every other weekend. But while Mark cherished the time together, for Geraldo it just served as a reminder that he had lost his family. His weekly visits soon became exercises in rage, and worse still he was beginning to unintentionally corrupt his younger brother. "Every time he'd come to visit we'd get into some kind of trouble," remembers Mark. "He would get in the worst fights with my mom about nothing, and then all he wanted to do was go raise hell. We'd go for a walk and the next thing I knew he was breaking a window or getting in a fight." Geraldo's anger finally pushed him well beyond his childish pranks and school yard brawls. When he was thirteen he joined a gang, and it was all downhill from there. By the time he was fourteen he had been arrested twice for petty theft and released with warnings and fines.

Then one weekend while visiting with his brother he convinced his younger sibling to help him steal a car. "We were just sitting on the lawn and he says, 'Let's go heist a car,' " recalls Mark. "I thought he was kidding. But the next thing I know I'm sitting in a stolen Camaro." Geraldo and Mark didn't get very far. Police caught them only a few blocks away. As it turns out the car belonged to an off-duty police officer. "I guess the worst part of all of that was seeing how terrified my little brother was," remembers Geraldo. "I felt so bad about what I did, but not for my-self—I didn't care about myself at all anymore, just for him." Geraldo confessed to the judge that the idea was all his and asked that his brother be dismissed. The judge believed his admission of guilt and let Mark go with a stern warning. But as for Geraldo, his record of violence and mayhem prompted the judge to order him into a juvenile correctional institute for three months.

Geraldo had forty-eight hours before he had to report to the detention center so Mark decided to use the time to give him a gift that would stay with both of them for the rest of their lives. He took his brother to a tattoo parlor where they bought tattoos that read BRO. "I figured that was the only way I could always be with him. I wanted him to know I was there for him all the time," says Mark.

The three hard months in detention changed Geraldo for the worse. He refused all visits from his mother. When he came out, he was, for all intents and purpose, a criminal. Now his gang ties were stronger than ever, and any hope for his rehabilitation was dashed when he learned that, because of his trouble, all visitation with his brother would be off-limits. Worse still, his mother decided a drastic change of location and environment was necessary to protect Mark from falling prey to the same forces which she thought had corrupted Geraldo. She decided to accept a post with her church as a missionary in Africa and the boys' parents agreed that Mark would accompany her. Again, both boys were stunned and hurt. "She meant well," says Mark. "But she didn't realize that what she was doing was killing us both." Like before, Geraldo reacted to the news with violence. The next day he was arrested with his hoodlum friends for mugging a delivery driver and stealing $150. The fact that one of the gang held a gun meant this time things were much more grave. For his involvement Geraldo was sentenced to two years, not to be released until he was eighteen years old.

Mark came to see his brother behind bars where he renewed their solemn promise. "He told me that no matter what happened he would always be there for me in his heart," says Geraldo. "I could see in his eyes how sincere he was, and it meant a lot to me." But remarkably that was the last time the two brothers would speak for almost six years.

Soon after that emotional meeting, Mark's mother moved the boy from Chicago halfway around the world to the outskirts of Nairobi, Africa, for two years of service. While Mark gained an education in international affairs and culture as well as the freedom to study and learn unobstructed by the street violence that Geraldo had become a part of, his brother became a hardened criminal.

When Geraldo was released from prison, his brother and mother prepared to return from their mission. Geraldo wrote one last letter to his brother telling him of his plans not to return home with his father, instead deciding to live with some gang friends. "That was terrifying because I knew it meant that he decided to devote his life to the gangs and to crime," remembers Mark. "That's the first time I really thought my brother was going to be killed in some kind of gang shoot-out for sure." By the time that Geraldo's letter made it all the way to Africa, he had already been released from jail and disappeared into the inner city gang culture. When Mark returned to United States his brother was nowhere to be found.

Mark moved to Florida to study psychology before graduating at the top of his class and becoming a social counselor. Geraldo drifted in and out of trouble, just barely managing to stay out of jail and sending an occasional card to Mark but never with a return address. "He would tell me he was working here or there, but no specifics," says Mark. "I hoped he was alright and when he was ready he would come around. I missed him so much." The semester before Mark graduated he went home to Chicago to spend the summer with his dad and work with an urban support center on curbing gang violence. His job was to go out into the community and find gang members he thought could be turned from the lifestyle and bring them into the center.

Then one fateful night, an eleven-year-old gang member Mark was trying to dissuade from a life of crime called him from a pay phone terrified because his gang brothers were trying to force him to join them in holding up a local convenience store at gunpoint. "This kid was so scared," reveals Mark. "He didn't want to do this, but he was afraid to turn them down." Even though it was almost midnight Mark rushed over to help his young friend. When the gang showed up to enlist their little friend's support one of the members looked strangely familiar to Mark. Then he noticed the tattoo on his arm that read BRO! It was his brother, Geraldo. The scars on his face and body along with the shaved head made him almost unrecognizable, but there was no mistaking the tattoo or the tears in his eyes when he saw Mark. "It truly opened my heart again when I saw my brother. I thought I was dead inside but the second I saw him looking so good and there to help that little kid, it made me feel like there was hope for me," remembers Geraldo.

Mark begged Geraldo to come home with him. At first Geraldo refused, but when he grabbed his brother and hugged him, Geraldo finally gave in. The two men and the youngster headed off together to a diner for something to eat, and afterward Mark brought them both back to Mark and Geraldo's dad's house where their father greeted Geraldo with tears of joy. But hard-hearted Geraldo made it quite clear that this night was not the end of his life of crime. "I really believed I belonged on the streets," says Geraldo. "When we went to bed that night I told them I wouldn't be there in the morning when they woke up."

The next day Geraldo was gone as he promised and Mark returned to work at the center with his new young friend. When he arrived, the place was abuzz with bad news. There was a shoot-out and men were dead—the same men Geraldo and the young boy were about to join in a holdup before Mark rescued them. The gang that went to hold up the convenience store got held up by some rival gang members just a few minutes after they robbed the store. Shots were fired and two were dead. "Being with my brother that night saved his life," declares Mark. "Now more than ever I just wanted to talk with him and show him the proof of why he couldn't go on this way."

Mark didn't have to wait long to make his case. His brother who had just heard the same news came to pay a visit. He walked up to Mark and collapsed into his brother's arms, crying like a baby. He was ready to change and ready to love his family once again. "I knew he had saved my life, and I knew there must be a reason for that," reveals Geraldo. "Seeing how he had done so good with that boy the night before really touched me inside. I figured I'd give him a chance to help me. And I knew he was my only hope. I had to put my trust in him."

Mark got Geraldo off the streets and into a program to stop the violence and get his life back together. Within a year he had healed the rift between himself and his mother. And today both boys are working as missionaries bringing their lessons of love to troubled people around the world. "We never gave up on each other," says Mark. "That's the secret of our success. And that's what we try to teach and bring to people in other countries and all over the world. We are all brothers and sisters everywhere in the world, and we all must be determined not to give up on each other either."

Love After Death

$\sim$

*L*awrence was a mischievous kid with more than his share of behavior problems until his father took him by the hand and heart and got him on the straight and narrow. "I was kind of a troublemaker kid," admits Lawrence. "But my dad was a natural-born psychologist, and he knew what I needed and how to give it to me. He was always there to talk to. He never allowed me to feel like I was alone in my problems." His dutiful dad stood by him through thick and thin every day of his life.

A hairdresser by trade, Lawrence's dad ran a salon in Fort Worth, Texas, with wife, Patsy, while they cared for their two young boys. Years of listening to customers' life stories while they sat in his salon chair getting their hair done taught him to be sensitive to people's feelings. That skill came in handy when the caring and attentive dad realized his son Lawrence was a little bit of a rebel who liked fast motorcycles and doing the opposite of whatever he was told. But most of all he knew his son needed something to keep him occupied and out of trouble. So he suggested motocross as a sport. "I loved it," says Lawrence. "And it kept me focused on something constructive and positive. Plus, it gave my dad and me a nice way to spend some time together. He was my best friend."

From that day on Lawrence's dad spent as much time as he could with his son teaching him about motorcycles and taking him to races all over Texas on weekends. As father and son became closer and closer, Lawrence grew up to make his parents proud by joining the army and eventually becoming a pilot. "He's the kind of son who always let us know with his words and actions that he loved and appreciated us as parents," says his mom, Patsy. "I know that's because his dad always taught him to care about people and not to be afraid of showing his emotions. That's the gift that his father had."

Young Lawrence went on to have his own family—three little girls and a sweet and loving wife of his own—passing that gift of love and sensitivity he received from his dad onto his own family. And as Lawrence's parents adjusted to having the house to themselves when their two boys went out on their own, Lawrence's father retired from the salon and started working as a handyman helping out friends and other needy people in the community. "He just loved people," remembers Patsy. "He wanted to pitch in however he could."

Lawrence's father always tried to be a positive and healing influence in the lives of others. So it was just par for the course when one day he came home from getting his driver's license renewed to tell his wife that he had registered as an organ donor. "He asked me what if it was one of our sons or someone we knew that needed an organ to survive?" remembers Patsy. " 'We have to think of the living after we're gone,' he told me." His father realized that he could save a life after he died and he wanted to do it. For Lawrence it was just another perfect example of the caregiver dad he knew so well and loved. "It was so natural for him to want to help anyone he could in whatever way he could," says Lawrence. "He had a real heart, and he cared about people even if he didn't really know them that well."

Meanwhile Lawrence was literally on top of the world when he retired from the military to be a commercial pilot. But something suddenly wasn't right. He started feeling weak. An incredibly athletic and fit man, he was disturbed when he began having trouble catching his breath after his morning runs. When his legs mysteriously started swelling up he knew it was time to get a check-up.

At first doctors dismissed Lawrence's condition as a myriad of unimportant symptoms. Some even told him there was nothing wrong. Then out of nowhere came a terrifying diagnosis—he had somehow contracted hepatitis C while overseas in the military and his liver was destroyed. His only hope would be a transplant. "I couldn't understand any of this," remembers Lawrence. "My whole life was on the line here. And there was nothing I could do about it. They told me I could die." Lawrence was placed on the register as a candidate for a new liver, but it was a long list. And the odds of him receiving a liver in time to save his life were slim to none.

As Lawrence tried to hang on, his devastated parents tried everything they could to help. As they both did their best to lend moral support for their son, Lawrence grew weaker and weaker. While on oxygen his skin became yellow, he lost forty pounds, and he was as frail as an old man. Doctors couldn't say how much time he had left while machines kept him alive. "I knew I was dying, and I didn't know what to do. I figured this was the end," reveals Lawrence.

Now Lawrence's father could only pray and hope that someone who met with a tragic end had thought to be as kind and helpful as he was when he registered as a donor earlier that year. But that wasn't all—they would have to be an exact match as well. His parents tried to carry on with their lives ever hopeful for their son's recovery.

Then one day Lawrence's father left the house to help someone out who couldn't afford to have her roof fixed. But at the end of the day he still hadn't returned, so his concerned wife, Patsy, went out looking for him. She was shocked to find her husband sitting on the curb dazed and confused in front of the house he was fixing. "He was really out of it, but he couldn't tell me what was wrong or why he was feeling so sick. He didn't have any memory of anything that happened that day," says Patsy. Patsy helped her husband into the car and headed for home when he told her he needed to go to the hospital. "He just knew that he had to go get some help," she said. "I didn't know what was wrong, but I figured better safe than sorry." At the hospital, doctors determined the bruises on his head indicated that he had suffered some type of head injury and they hypothesized that he may have fallen off the roof he was working on earlier in the day, but they had no way of knowing for sure how the injuries were sustained.

They proceeded to treat him, and then tragedy struck. The next time Patsy saw her husband, he was in a coma. "It all happened so fast, and it was terrifying and confusing," says Patsy. "It didn't make any sense. One minute he was just a little dizzy and the next he was in a coma. I didn't know what to do." Sadly, only a few hours later Patsy's husband, and Lawrence's father, the man who had been a loving and supportive husband and dad for all those years, was dead. Apparently the mysterious injury had crushed his brain stem and by the time doctors realized the extent of the damage it was too late. Patsy was devastated. How could this happen? She was just talking to him a few hours before. She was just holding him and telling him that everything was alright. What went wrong? It was a horrible disaster that she couldn't comprehend.

But as she sat sobbing and trying to understand, the doctors informed her of yet another strange and incredible development. Her dead husband could now save her sick son. Tests were being done as they spoke to confirm that her husband was a perfect match to donate his liver to Lawrence. "There was nothing I could do to bring my husband back to life," says Patsy. "But at least maybe he could now save our son. It would have been unbearable to lose both of them." But there wasn't a moment to lose. The tests would have to be completed. Even though they were father and son there was still only a fifty-fifty chance that the organ was a perfect match.

But when all was said and done it was confirmed that his father had the liver that could save his son's life. His father's death had happened so fast that doctors were forced to tell Lawrence the news of his father's death and his life-saving gift in the same breath. "It was real tough hearing both those things at the same time," says Lawrence. "Losing my dad was the worst thing I've ever felt in my entire life, worse than hearing about my own possible death. But to hear that the last thing he was going to do was to give me my life back was as if he was reaching out to me from beyond the grave to tell me how much he loved me. But there was no way to thank him anymore." Surgeons rushed

Lawrence into the operating room, and two hours and twenty-two minutes later Lawrence's father was now a permanent part of him. His father's healthy liver was now what was keeping his son alive. "I was heartbroken over my father's death," says Lawrence, "but I never felt so close to him as I did at that moment. He saved my life—what greater gift can a son get from a father?"

Meanwhile for Lawrence's mother the fact that she was spared the grief of losing a son because her husband made a decision to care was her only solace after losing her husband so tragically. "We were married forty-five years, and I loved my husband more than anything," says Patsy. "This is the only thing that has saved me mentally. I have a feeling my husband is watching over us and he's happy knowing what happened."

But Lawrence wasn't the only one his father saved. In addition to his son, his thoughtfulness saved two other people with his healthy kidney donations, which gave his son even more to be proud of and left a legacy of love that Lawrence will never forget. "He's my hero," says his son. "Throughout his life and finally when he died, he really showed me how important it was to think of others."

Love in a Bottle

Colby was only six years old in the fall of 1972 when he came home from school one day and heard the shocking news that his father was missing in action in Vietnam and presumed dead. For Colby, it was like the end of the world. "My dad was everything to me. He was my best friend, my teacher, my basketball coach, the guy who made me feel important, you name it," remembers Colby. "I couldn't even understand life without him." He was devastated by the loss and sank into a deep depression that neither his mother, Gina, his teachers, nor his friends could dispel.

The one-time perfect student began failing at all his classes, lost his appetite, and rarely wanted to play with his friends anymore. His mother tried everything from long talks and loving hugs to toys and fancy gifts to help her son recover. Living in Chicago, she once even blew a bundle on two courtside seats for herself and her basketball-fan son to see his favorite team, the Bulls, play up close and personal, hoping it would lift his spirits. But it only reminded Colby of how he used to watch the games with his dad, and he quietly wept through the whole game.

That summer after the school year ended, Colby's mother took her son on a trip across country in an effort to bring Colby out of his funk. Mother and son packed up her Mustang and headed out on the open road. Over the next month they traveled the highways and back roads of America. Gina tried everything she could to be the father Colby had lost. But no matter how hard she tried, he just grew more and more withdrawn. "Here she was giving me this opportunity that most kids would have died for—to see the country," says Colby. "But I was angry. I wanted to see my dad, just to say goodbye if nothing else. I felt cheated that I never had that chance." As the two reached Los Angeles and the Pacific Ocean, Gina grabbed her son by the hand and ran him down to the beach. She hoped the mighty ocean would have enough water in it to wash away her son's tears.

As they walked along the shore, Colby's mom suddenly had an idea she thought would help her son get over his dad's death. "She asked me what I would say to my dad if I could tell him anything I wanted," remembers Colby. "I was blown away because that's exactly what I was thinking about. So I told her I wanted to tell him that I loved him and goodbye until I saw him in heaven." Gina took her son down the street to the corner liquor store and bought a bottle of wine, asking the owner to remove the cork. Then they walked back to the beach and she dumped out the wine in the surf. She took a pen and piece of stationery from her purse and handed it to Colby instructing him to write his dad a letter. Colby addressed the letter to his father properly just as if he were really sending a letter, then he followed his father's name with the words, "Somewhere in Vietnam." He wrote everything he wanted to tell his dad. When her son was finished, Gina took the letter and placed it in the bottle and sealed it with the cork nice and solid. Then she grabbed her son's hand and ran him out to the edge of the nearby pier. "She told me to kiss the bottle and say goodbye," remembers Colby. "Then I threw it as far as I could. The second I did I felt better, and it brought me closer than ever to my mom because I knew she understood what I needed."

Two weeks later mother and son returned to their home and lives back in Chicago. Gina went back to school and found a job as a teacher and Colby slowly made his way out of his depression. He became a star basketball player in high school and went on to college on a scholarship, eventually becoming a child psychologist. The bottle and the memorable summer became only a pleasant and distant memory.

Colby grew into a fine and responsible young man who would have made his father proud. He became a counselor at a high school in Chicago where he earned a reputation for handling problem cases well. "Losing my dad when I was a kid really gave me tremendous insight into the kinds of emotions that can make a child rebel or withdraw from society," says Colby. "That helped me a great deal in understanding and helping what others considered problem students."

In the spring of 1986, a very special student walked into Colby's office. Nguyen was a young Vietnamese boy whose father also died during the Vietnamese conflict. Nguyen's father gave up his life to save his family when he jumped on a live grenade that flew into their home during a fire fight between U.S. and Vietcong troops. Nguyen was just a baby when his father died, and his mother fled with the rest of the family for the refuge of America in 1975 after the fall of Saigon. After a short stay in Seattle, Washington, they moved to Chicago. Now a high school freshman who had a long history of trouble in school, he was failing his classes and seemed to have no interest in improving.

As Colby began to get to know Nguyen he found out more and more about the young man's family and where they were from. Colby knew many of the cities and landmarks that Nguyen described from his father's letters home. He shared the story of his father and how he lost him during the same war. "I could tell that he trusted me more as soon as he knew that I also lost my father in Vietnam," says Colby. "I shared everything I could about my dad and how he died. I wasn't going to hold back anything from him. The more I shared, the more he did." Colby came to the conclusion that he had a great deal in common with his young friend. And just maybe he knew how to help. "Part of the reason he was so angry and sad wasn't because his dad was killed but because he never got to tell him he loved him," explains Colby. "He finally confessed to me that he always wished he had a chance to thank his dad for giving up his life for him."

Convinced that Nguyen had spent most of his life suffering the same feelings that Colby experienced so many years before, he thought he'd try the same solution. He told Nguyen all about what he had done on the beach years before with the bottle. Then he suggested that Nguyen write down all those things that he wanted to tell his dad but never got a chance to say and seal them in a bottle to toss into Lake Michigan. "It was a long shot, but if it worked for me, I thought it was worth a shot," says Colby.

Nguyen loved the idea. In fact he was so excited about doing it that he told his mom what he has planned to do. When he did, his mother couldn't believe her ears. She

immediately called Colby with an unbelievable revelation—
she had found Colby's bottle on a beach years earlier. "She
asked me if my dad was a staff sergeant," reveals Colby.
"Then she told me exactly what I wrote in the letter. It
was like a *Twilight Zone* episode. It was just too weird."
Colby couldn't understand how what she was saying was
possible, but when she explained it all it made sense.
Nguyen's mother, Thanh, found the bottle on the beaches
of Seattle where she and her family were living in 1977
when they first arrived in the United States. Somehow the
bottle had floated up the West Coast of the United States
in the five years since Colby heaved it into the Pacific in
Los Angeles back in 1972. When Nguyen's mom read the
moving letter from a little boy who lost his father with the
address reading, "Somewhere in Vietnam," it touched her
heart and made an indelible impression. "I felt so afraid
and alone in my pain when we first got to this country,"
says Thanh. "But when I found the bottle it was like a sign
that I was supposed to be here, and that we weren't the
only ones suffering. I realized my son was not the only boy
who lost a father. Somehow that made it easier."

Thanh threw the bottle back into the ocean after reading
the letter hoping it would inspire anyone else who found
it just as it had encouraged her, and she never shared the
experience with Nguyen who was just four years old at the
time. After Colby overcame his shock, he realized that his
mother's act of love had reached out to someone else half

a country away and made a difference. "It was the love of a mother, father, and a son all rolled up in one and sent out to the rest of the world," says Colby.

A few days later Colby, Nguyen, and his mother stood together on the shore and tossed a bottle into Lake Michigan—this one filled with everything Nguyen wanted to tell his dad. And over the next few months Colby worked closely with him to bring up his grades. Nguyen slowly but surely came around and eventually graduated and went on to join the Peace Corps.

Now Colby says the bottle means far more than it did that day he threw it into the ocean. "It's like my dad answered that letter through the people who found it," says Colby. "And he's telling me that he's proud of how I turned out. I love you, Dad, wherever you are."

A Giant Step for Love

〜

*L*aura and Chris met while working their way through college in Pennsylvania and it was a storybook romance. He was a lifeguard when he wasn't in school and she was a cheerleader. They fell in love at first sight and figured they'd settle down, get married, and have a baby. They were smart, healthy, crazy about each other, and they were determined to have the perfect family.

The lovebirds moved in together and Laura quit school and went to work to help pay for Chris to finish college and become a teacher. Then he reciprocated by working two jobs to put her through college so she could achieve her dream of becoming a nurse. "We were a real team and we worked hard to help each other however we could," remembers Laura. She finally graduated college and realized her dream of becoming a critical care nurse. The two married soon after.

Their storybook romance continued as Laura and Chris decided it was time to put step two of their plan into action and to have a child. "We were both where we wanted to be in our lives, and we figured it was time to have our dream of a nice little family come true," remembers Laura. She became pregnant and carried their child with the same devotion and dedication she had toward the rest of their relationship. "I did everything I was supposed to," recalls Laura. "I wanted that child to be the healthiest it could be." She stopped drinking, didn't smoke, exercised regularly, and she ate nothing but healthy food. She was the perfect picture of pregnancy.

But as the due date approached Laura didn't feel right. "I just knew there was something wrong," remembers Laura. "I had a very bad feeling." Laura checked into the hospital for testing and discovered the worst. Tests confirmed their unborn child was lying on his umbilical cord and cutting off his own oxygen supply. Their precious baby was slowly being asphyxiated. "One minute we were the happiest people in the world, the next minute we knew our baby could die," says Laura. Doctors ordered an emergency cesarean section to try and save the baby. But when they pulled him from Laura's belly he was blue and breathless. "My six-foot-tall husband fainted the second he saw him," reveals Laura. "I just cried. It was nothing that either of us ever could have been prepared for."

But their devoted doctor refused to give up and immediately began performing CPR. The doctor worked feverishly to save the child. Then precious seconds later that dedication paid off when the sweet sound of a crying baby filled the room with happiness and Laura's and Chris's hearts with renewed hope. "I gave my baby a quick kiss on the forehead and then they rushed him away to try and keep him alive," says Laura. The baby was alive, but the diagnosis was grim. Doctors doubted the child would survive the night. "Our doctor told us we had to name our son immediately because he might be dead in a few hours," says Laura. "It just shakes you to the core to hear such a thing." They named their new baby Kyle and they were determined that he would live.

But the injuries caused by the oxygen deprivation were extremely serious and extensive. His lungs were damaged, his heart was enlarged, he suffered ruptured kidneys, and a host of other ailments not even fully known yet. While Kyle lay in a respirator barely hanging on to life, Laura was given strict orders to remain in bed and recover from her surgery, but it was impossible to keep her from her child. "Just as soon as they would get me back in the bed I'd sneak down to the infant intensive care unit to see him," says Laura. "I had to be with him. I knew it would give him strength to see me." Laura and Chris no longer cared about having the perfect baby, now they just wanted this one to live.

Finally after weeks of waiting, the news was good. Kyle would survive and he was now eating and breathing on his own. They sent him home with his parents on a monitor to detect epileptic seizures, yet another complication of his condition. The prognosis still wasn't very promising though. Laura and Chris would simply have to wait and see how Kyle's condition unfolded before they truly knew what his life would be like. But one thing was for sure—they weren't giving up on their son. "No matter what doctors told us we knew he was going to make it," says Laura. "He was a fighter." Three months later doctors finally made a diagnosis—their son had neuromuscular cerebral palsy. He would never walk and he would be plagued by a lifetime of mental and physical challenges.

Kyle's parents heard the dooming diagnosis, but they decided their child would do what doctors said he couldn't. "We loved him regardless of whether he could walk or not, but we weren't going to believe in doctors. We believed in Kyle and when you looked into his eyes, you knew he didn't want to give up," declares Laura. Chris supplemented his income as a teacher by going back to work on the side as a lifeguard while Laura continued working as a nurse in order to keep up with the incredible costs of medical care and insurance. And Chris and Laura poured their hearts into their child feeding him all the positive energy they could. "We even set up a crib in the lifeguard house on the weekends for Kyle so we could both be with him when Chris was working," says Laura. "He saw his dad save a lot of lives there." Every day the couple hoped for a breakthrough or a cure of some sort.

Meanwhile Kyle proved he was a indeed a fighter. Doctors put braces on his legs to straighten them and prevent further muscular damage, but Kyle was soon struggling to stand despite the excruciating pain. Still Kyle wouldn't settle for that. "He wanted to walk so bad, and he wasn't going to give up trying not even when we told him it was alright to stop and take a break," remembers Laura.

Two years later Laura and Chris received some extraordinary news that there was a new medical procedure that might enable Kyle to walk. But the revolutionary procedure involved multiple painful surgeries and a long and difficult rehabilitation effort. Laura and Chris weren't ready to put their five-year-old son through such an ordeal unless he really wanted it. "We thought it was important that he make the decision one way or another," remembers Laura. "He looked up at me with that beautiful smile and said he wanted to walk and be like other kids. We decided to help make his wish come true." They went ahead with the elaborate operation, which involved surgically stretching his tendons and muscles in a way that would counteract the damage that had occurred at birth. The surgeries were successful but the real work was yet to come. It would take years of painful rehabilitation and all Kyle's sheer strength and determination to develop his muscles. "I could see in his eyes how bad he was hurting through it all," recalls Laura. "Yet he refused to ever give in to the pain. He wanted so badly to walk, there was nothing that was going to hold him back. I just wished I could take that pain away."

When Laura and Chris heard about some very gifted therapists at Children's Specialized Hospital in Toms River, New Jersey, who were part of the famed Children's Miracle Network they decided to contact them. From the moment they walked in the front door, they knew this was where Kyle belonged. "They believed that he could walk, and they cared about Kyle enough to be gentle with him," remembers Laura.

The devoted therapists took a uniquely personal approach to Kyle's therapy. They quickly got to know Kyle and they used that personal knowledge to inspire and encourage him. Once they knew what Kyle was thinking and feeling, they worked with Laura and Chris to devise a customized plan of therapy. "He loved basketball, for instance, so they started throwing a ball back and forth to him." explains Laura. "They knew he had a lot of anger inside of him because of his condition so they encouraged him to take the anger out with props like throwing items against the wall or even at us or squeezing down on clamps as hard as he could." The personality approach was helping bring out the person inside Kyle, the little boy who wanted to walk so much but didn't know how to do it.

As he struggled to stand with the help of a walker and take his first awkward and painful steps since the surgery, the therapists and even Laura and Chris learned more about their son Kyle and what he was feeling and thinking. That led them to a rather surprising breakthrough. There was one thing Kyle wanted almost as bad as being able to walk—a trip to Disney World! "The truth is we hadn't really ever been on a vacation since Kyle was born because we were so focused on his medical care," reveals Laura. "We never realized how much he wanted to go to Disney World."

As Kyle continued to improve despite the pain, his parents thought of the perfect reward for his hard work. As an incentive, they told him as soon as he could walk across the room, they would take him to Disney World. "Twenty steps is what we told him," explains Laura. "That was the magic number. We knew he'd do it. But we were ready to wait a while for it to happen. We needed time to save up for the trip anyway." Laura and Chris believed in their son, but even if he couldn't walk the full twenty steps they were ready to make his dream come true. Now they could only wait and see.

But before they even had time to put away the first dollar for the trip, Kyle had his eye on the prize. Inspired by the promise of Disney World, Kyle was making it halfway across the room just a few days later. "We were astonished," reveals Laura. "His whole demeanor changed. He was happy, and he was walking like it was easy. It was still just a few steps or so, but even this was more than the first doctors ever said was possible." Within just another month his devoted therapists happily stood by Kyle's parents while he walked not just five or ten, but twenty steps! "It was unbelievable, we didn't even have the money saved up yet for the trip," says Laura. "We had to take out a loan."

That month Kyle made his two dreams come true at once by walking on his own two feet through the turnstiles at Disney World for the first time in his life. As he glanced out at the thousands of other children there that day, for the first time ever Kyle didn't feel left out of life. "The smile he had on his face started at his heart and came out his eyes," remembers Laura. "He knew he won his fight."

Since then Kyle has progressed by leaps and bounds instead of steps, and is literally running as fast as he can to catch up with his future.

Guilty on All Counts of Love!

The diploma on the wall called Jeff a lawyer but by his own admission he was really a con man and a crook with no intention of ever mending his ways. "I was just about the crookedest lawyer I knew," admits Jeff. "I was proud of that too." Jeff was a criminal defense lawyer who made a fortune defending guilty clients with underhanded tactics. And though his ill-gotten gain delivered him right into the lap of luxury, it also landed him in a heap of trouble.

Growing up, Jeff never really wanted to make a living the old-fashioned way—by earning it. Instead he was always looking for the easy way out and dreaming up some way to cheat the system. He found that out in college while working on a term paper in his freshman history class on the American criminal justice system. "The paper was supposed to teach us how the presumption of innocence was the bedrock of the American legal system, but that's not what I saw," reveals Jeff. "I learned the amount of money paid to defense attorneys each year in this country was staggering." Jeff saw a system whereby a crooked lawyer could make a bundle of money by successfully defending the wealthiest and most guilty clients he could find, and now he knew that was the job for him.

After graduating with his law degree, he pursued his plan to the fullest to save America's criminals and get rich. He opened up his own practice in a major Midwestern city and immediately began frequenting the police precincts looking for rich crooks who needed a good lawyer fast. "I figured I could charge those suckers as much as I wanted," reveals Jeff. "Double the bill, triple the bill—it didn't matter because they knew they were guilty and they didn't care what they paid as long as I got them off." Overcharging was an art form for Jeff—knowing just exactly how high he could go without out-pricing a client. But that was just the tip of the iceberg. He routinely resorted to activities practically as criminal as those committed by his clients. As soon as Jeff had a client onboard he'd sometimes raise the price as much as five to ten times the original estimate without even notifying them. If they refused to pay, he'd make sure they lost the case. "It was extortion," admits Jeff. "Without a doubt what I was doing was illegal and wholly unethical. I would have been disbarred in a minute if anyone blew the whistle on me. But I was damn good in the courtroom, and I believed I would never get caught. Plus, I was making ungodly amounts of money."

Jeff's improprieties weren't limited to his client relations either. If Jeff couldn't win a case on the merit of his evidence and arguments, he was never above buying the evidence he needed, and of course charging the client for the illegally obtained information. "I knew every bad cop on the force," says Jeff. "And the ones that weren't crooked probably became crooked after they met me. I was very convincing."

But Jeff's law-breaking lifestyle didn't come without a price. Though on the surface he pretended not to care, on the inside Jeff was dying of guilt. He had alienated just about everybody close to him, including his own mother who threatened to completely disown him unless he changed his ways. "They all knew I was a criminal, and I knew it, too, so I just became this miserable person to be around," admits Jeff. "I hated myself. But I was addicted to the money and the rush of winning." Hard-hearted Jeff even once jokingly threatened to kill his mother if she didn't stop bothering him about his crooked ways. "I was kidding of course, but it was a sick and horrible thing to say even as a joke," admits Jeff. His mother was not amused by his sick sense of humor, yet still she tried to get through to her son and help him to see the error of his ways. But

Jeff would have none of her "hokey wisdom," as he put it. He slowly began distancing himself from his mother until finally he no longer even spoke to her.

By the time he was thirty-three years old, Jeff had everything he wanted—money, power and success—everything but peace of mind. And that's when it all began to slip away. One fall morning, his uncle phoned and woke him up to let him know his mom was dying. She was in the advanced stages of breast cancer. Suddenly Jeff was beginning to feel something he never knew he could feel—regret. "I had told her over and over again how I didn't give a damn about what she thought of me, but the truth couldn't have been further off," says Jeff. "I loved her and I felt so ashamed and guilty."

Jeff went to the hospital to visit his mother and as always Jeff tried to act detached. He showered her with gifts—everything from flowers to jewelry, but she wanted none of it. She only had one request, and that was for him to change his life. She asked him to start by using his law degree to help poor people. "She was on chemo and I thought all the drugs were going to her head," says Jeff. "Here she is dying and she tells me she wants me to start doing work for free for homeless people and stuff like that. I thought she was nuts." But despite how many times he tried to change the subject, his mother kept bringing it back up until finally he promised he would do what she asked. "I told her that just to shut her up," says Jeff. "But I had no intention of following through with it."

Jeff left the hospital and returned the next day to visit his mother again but was shocked when he learned his mother had passed away while he was on his way there. The cancer and the painful chemotherapy had taken its toll on her weak heart. But Jeff couldn't help feeling like he had killed her. "Down deep I knew if I had been a kinder son, she probably would have lived longer than she did," reveals Jeff. "There was nothing I could do to ever change that or bring her back now." But then he realized there was something that he could do to honor his mother, even after her death.

Amazingly, hard-hearted Jeff decided that day to fulfill his mother's request that he help the poor and homeless. He immediately contacted several of the local shelters and agreed to do pro bono legal work on behalf of some of the displaced people who had routine run-ins with the law. He promised to spend one afternoon a month at the shelter. "I didn't know how long this would last or if I'd actually be able to help anybody, but I had to do it for my mom," says Jeff.

Every trip to the mission changed Jeff a little. Suddenly he was asking himself why these innocent people were so forgotten and why dishonest people like himself were allowed to have so much. "At first I tried convincing myself that it wasn't my problem, that only the strong survive and all that nonsense," explains Jeff. "But you just can't look into a starving kid's eyes and tell him that. The children really got to me." And as Jeff's heart began to soften to the plight of the underprivileged people he was helping, he grew more and more unhappy about the life he was living.

Soon Jeff's health began to deteriorate. Before long he was in the doctor's office three times a month with various gastrointestinal disorders. "I was miserable," says Jeff. "I knew it was because I felt so guilty about all the people I'd hurt over the years, but I still couldn't give up the life I had devoted myself to. Plus there was still all that money." But though Jeff wasn't ready to change his life yet, forces beyond his control were going to change it for him.

After getting a client cleared of an assault-and-battery charge by paying off the arresting officer to change his testimony, the injured party hired a private detective who uncovered the payoff. And as simply and quickly as that Jeff was in hot water. A few weeks later the situation snow-balled out of control and suddenly Jeff was under arrest and facing certain disbarment and jail time. When he heard the clang of the cell door closing behind him, everything became crystal clear to him. Jeff pleaded guilty in a deal with prosecutors to stay out of jail. "I had to give it all up," says Jeff. "I knew it was time to go straight." He was disbarred and never allowed to practice law again. Furthermore, he paid over $200,000 in fines and legal fees.

Now Jeff was out of jail, but he was also out of a job, out of money and had no idea what he was going to do to make a living. Nevertheless, he knew he did the right thing. "I felt my mom was happy now wherever she was," admits Jeff. "But it was like starting all over again. I didn't know where to go with my life." As Jeff struggled with the future, his present financial situation only grew worse. He sold his house and furniture to pay his debts and moved to a tiny studio apartment without any furniture. He was broke and alone in the world.

Then while shopping for groceries one day, he received help from the last place he ever expected—a homeless man asking him for a handout. Accustomed to usually telling them to get lost, this time he didn't. Instead, he asked the man if he knew of a shelter. When the man said no, Jeff volunteered to take him to one. "I never did anything like that before in my life," explains Jeff. "I figured why not help the guy out. I certainly didn't have any appointments that afternoon. As soon as I offered he got a big smile on his face. I hadn't felt that good in a long time." Jeff and his new friend hopped into his car and headed off for the shelter where Jeff used to donate his time. He hadn't been there in months since all of his problems unfolded. But as soon as he walked through the front door he was greeted with a warm reception. "The guy who ran the place, Joe, just grabbed me and gave me a big hug," says Jeff. "Then a bunch of people I'd helped came up and shook my hand. I was stunned."

Though Jeff didn't know it, the work he had done with the homeless shelter went a long way to making a difference. Because of Jeff's pro bono work, a mother got her son out of prison, a young girl was allowed to keep her baby until she got back on her feet, and an elderly man was able to prove his inheritance and wound up giving half the money to the shelter. Jeff sat and talked for hours with Joe and the homeless as they came and went. Then Joe made Jeff an unexpected proposal. "He asked me if I wanted a job as a full-time counselor," reveals Jeff. "In a thousand years I never could have seen myself doing that until that moment. I knew it was my calling. I took the job on the spot."

Fifteen years and thousands of hot meals later, Jeff has become an inspired and tireless advocate for the homeless. And his life couldn't be better. "My mom saved my life with her dying wish," says Jeff. "I'll never stop loving her for that or give up on honoring her memory by helping these people. Thanks Mom!"

Recovering Love

*J*ohn's parents owned a successful chain of retail stores in Dallas, Texas, but the wealthy entrepreneurs never spoiled their only child. They taught him the importance of values and the responsibility of those blessed with prosperity to pass that good fortune along in whatever way possible to the less fortunate. They told John that the world was one big family and that each member of that family had to pitch in and help the others.

His parents worked hard to be living examples of their words. When he was in grade school John's parents both gave of their time and money to local civic groups to help education programs for children, the homeless and the hungry. And every Thanksgiving, the family served hot meals at a shelter. "Some of my friends thought the

Thanksgiving thing was really going overboard, but it made me feel good helping those people even as a kid," remembers John.

John's parents' concern for others never waned even when they were on vacation. Every year John and his parents spent two weeks during the summer in the exotic tropics of the Yucatan Peninsula in Mexico. His parents loved the culture and the warm weather. It was a nice relief from the pressures of their business and everyday life. But even while basking in the sunshine they wanted to be a positive influence, particularly to a young Mexican boy name Miguel.

Miguel was a quick-thinking, kind and smart ten-year-old boy living in terrible conditions when they first met him in the summer of 1976. He had all the tools one needed for success—ambition, intelligence, perseverance, charm and persuasiveness as well as rugged good looks. But he was dirt poor and homeless. "I was just a baby when we first met him," reveals John. "But I still remember how sad I was when I saw the little shack he lived in." Miguel's mother died when he was ten and his father refused to take responsibility for him. His grandmother took him in for a while, but when she died a year later, he was on his own. Yet the cagey youth survived by showing tourists around in exchange for a meal or a dollar or two. Conscientious Miguel helped visitors stay clear of dangerous areas and told them which foods were safe to eat while helping them to have a good time.

After John's parents encountered the dynamic and helpful young man, they decided to help him by bringing him money and clothes, books and newspapers as well as friendship and advice every time they visited. The savvy professionals also helped Miguel see how he could make a good living for himself if he took his tourism business a little more seriously and focused on it.

Gradually, they saw how all their assistance was paying off in a big way. "Every time we'd go down there he was looking a little better," remembers John. "He started growing his tourism business and before long he was treating us to dinner." By the time Miguel was twenty, with the help of his American friends, his small trade had grown by leaps and bounds enabling him to save up enough money to travel to Mexico City to start university. He went on to work his way through medical school and become a respected physician.

As John's parents grew older they stopped spending their summers in Mexico, wanting to stay closer to home for health reasons. Miguel continued to write his American friends always thanking them for what they did and just to say hello until he graduated medical school and lost touch with the thoughtful family.

Years later as John prepared to graduate from college in

Texas, he and some classmates traveled to Acapulco for one last wild week of college fun. While buzzing along a remote stretch of beach on ATCs with a friend named Susan, John's cycle spun out of control in the slippery surf flipping over and sending John flying backward and hitting his head on some coral. He was unconscious and badly bleeding. "I blacked out as soon as I hit the rocks," explains John. "I don't remember anything after that, but Susan says she just started screaming as loud as she could for help, but it was hopeless because we were in the middle of nowhere." Afraid to leave her friend, but equally afraid to move him for fear of causing more damage, she was petrified and confused.

Finally, Susan made the hard decision to head for help back in town, but that was over two hours away. "She figured she'd head for a hospital, but she had no idea where to go," says John. "I was losing a lot of blood and she was terrified she wouldn't make it back in time." Flustered and frantic, Susan raced in the direction of town unsure of just how long her friend could survive.

A half an hour into her journey, she stumbled across a small shack of a building with a tiny red cross on top. Not knowing what to expect from the shabby roadside outpost, but desperate for help, Susan pulled over and ran inside. She was shocked when a doctor emerged from the back. He was a well-dressed young man in spectacles, and spoke perfect English. He was ready and willing to help. After

Susan frantically explained the situation, the doctor grabbed his medical bag and his keys and seconds later they hurried off to John's side in the doctor's truck.

When they arrived twenty minutes later, they found that John's pulse was faint and his blood pressure was barely registering. "It was horrible," says Susan. "I thought for sure he was dead because he looked so pale." After determining that there was no spinal damage the doctor realized the greatest danger now was blood loss. The doctor went to work to stop the bleeding, first cleansing the wound as best as he could then suturing it as quickly as possible. He successfully stopped up the wound, but for how long he didn't know. What he did know was that he had to get John to the hospital immediately. The doctor and Susan carried John to the truck and then rushed him back to the city as fast as they could.

An hour and a half later John was in the emergency room still unconscious. "I had lost so much blood," says John. "When I arrived they said I was barely alive." Doctors hurried to fill John's body with units of whole blood and raise his blood pressure and pulse while performing a battery of tests to determine the extent of his injuries. While John battled for life the helpful doctor sat with Susan holding her hand and assuring her that John would survive. "He was so concerned about whether John lived or died, that he was tearing up every time I did," says Susan. "For somebody that just met him, it was strange to me how much he cared. But I figured he was a very committed doctor."

An hour later John regained consciousness and was out of danger. Susan and the doctor embraced then went to visit John. As they both walked into his hospital room together, John focused on the stranger's familiar charming smile. "Susan was telling me all about him and how he saved me," explains John. "But all I could think about was that I knew this guy from somewhere. Then it hit me—this was Miguel!"

Incredibly John was right. Standing before him was the poor homeless boy his parents had helped years ago all grown up. "I was in shock," remembers John. "I reached up and grabbed him to hug him, and then realized that he might not know it was me." But Miguel did know. Although John may have looked different than he did as a child, Miguel recognized John the moment Susan told him his last name. Miguel explained to John that he wound up at the out-of-the way clinic after leaving Mexico City to practice medicine in the poverty-stricken areas of the country where he felt he could really make a difference and help pass on some of the good fortune he received to the people of Mexico. But on this day John realized it was he who was receiving the good fortune. "The doctors at the hospital told me that if I hadn't been brought in when I was I would definitely have died or at the very least slipped into a coma," reveals John. "Without a doubt Miguel saved my life, and I will always be in his debt for that."

But to Miguel, helping John was the least he could do to pay back the family that gave him a life. "I never knew how to thank them for what they did for me," says Miguel. "They gave me help, friendship, and the idea that helping others was something important. If it wasn't for them, I wouldn't have been able to be there to help John."

Now John says he'll carry the lesson of his parents and the doctor who paid him back their kindness for the rest of his life. "Every night before I go to bed I ask myself if I helped somebody that day," says John. "If I can say yes, then I know I had a good day—if not then I make that my number one goal for the next day. And I sleep like a baby."

Don't Cat Around
with Love

~ ⌒ ⌒ ~

*J*enny had just lost her husband to colon cancer
and it was still a struggle for the fifty-nine-year-
old childless widow to stop crying before she left the house
everyday. But when she found a helpless kitten fighting for
its life after being hit by a car, she was ready and willing
to lend a hand. "At first I thought it was dead," reveals
Jenny. "But then it opened his eyes and looked at me so
sadly I had to help."

Jenny took the injured cat under her wing and rushed
him to the nearby animal rescue hospital. But with multiple
broken bones, a ruptured kidney and a punctured liver, he
didn't have much of a chance. They patched him as best
as they could and said that the kitten would need complex,
ongoing care and attention as well as multiple surgeries in

the future and costly medical treatments. They advised putting the cat to sleep, but Jenny wouldn't hear of it. "I just couldn't do it—not right after losing my husband," remembers Jenny. "All I had now was the memory of my husband and the money he left me. If I could use that money to help this cat, I just figured why not?"

Jenny adopted the fallen feline and named him Rudy after her husband. With her love and intense medical attention the cat slowly returned to health. A year later Rudy was on his paws and living as normal a life as possible. Most important he was a constant comfort to his savior, Jenny. "I loved that cat with all my heart," says Jenny. "He was my best friend. And he helped me get through that very rough period after my husband's death. I really don't know how I would have made it without him being there."

Now Jenny and Rudy were facing life day by day together. When Jenny cooked Rudy would jump up onto the counter to help. When she played the piano, Rudy would always lie down on the piano top ready to add a note or two by pouncing on the keys at just the right moment. And of course when it was time to turn in, Rudy knew his place was on the pillow right next to Jenny.

But despite Rudy's companionship, after a few years, Jenny felt ready to meet a man to share her time with— not a replacement for her husband, which she knew was impossible, but someone nice to talk with and dance with. But she was dumfounded over how to meet such a man.

All her girlfriends were happily married with big families and they didn't know either. Jenny was on her own when it came to the singles lifestyle.

So when her brother suggested she try out the local senior singles dances she decided to give it a shot. Jenny started going to the dances by herself, and she met one man after another. Some were nice and some were not. But none were really much to speak about.

In fact she was getting ready to quit going when she met Ronnie. "He swept me off my feet the night we met," says Jenny. "He seemed too good to be true, but he was just so nice and gentlemanly, he made me feel safe and secure." Ronnie was everything she missed in her husband. He was dashingly handsome. He was kind, sweet and thoughtful. When she told him how much she missed her husband's birthday cards, he began bringing her a card every time they'd get together. He did everything right. And even though Jenny barely knew him, within a month she was falling in love. She decided to invite him over to her house for the first time to cook him dinner.

Jenny was extremely nervous and excited that night. It was the first time she had cooked for a man since her husband. She went all out to make all her specialty dishes. She was dressed to the nines and ready for her Romeo when the door bell rang. But the second she opened the door for Mr. Right, something happened to Rudy. "He went crazy," says Jenny. "He was hissing and squealing as if I was tor-

turing him. He had never acted like that ever before."
Jenny tried to calm down her cat. But no matter how much
she tried to quell his screams, Rudy wouldn't stop. Finally
she was forced to lock him in the bedroom so she and
Ronnie could sit down to dinner.

Jenny had a nice time with Ronnie that night, but Rudy's
crying just wouldn't stop. When she tried to let Rudy out
of the room again after dinner to be with the two of them,
he immediately ran up to Ronnie and began hissing again.
When he tried to pet him, he laid a wallop of a scratch on
him. "I didn't know if it was his cologne or what, but he
was not liking him," says Jenny. "Finally, I thought maybe
it was just that he wasn't used to having another man in
the house besides himself."

Despite her cat's dislike of her suitor she continued to
see Ronnie. But when the wailing, hissing, and scratching
just wouldn't stop, the normally unsuspecting Jenny started
to wonder what was up. "I wasn't going to let my cat tell
me who I could see," says Jenny. "But it definitely did give
me pause for thought. I started thinking about what was
wrong with this guy. It made me a little more cautious."

Over the next few weeks Jenny continued to see Ronnie
and she fell deeper and deeper in love. But despite her
efforts to get to know him better she couldn't find out
much of anything about his past except that he was retired
and had recently relocated from San Diego. Yet he had
started putting on the pressure for Jenny to get serious fast.

Meanwhile, she was still trying to figure out a way to get her cat to like him.

So when Ronnie asked her to marry him just after two months, she became very uncomfortable. "He popped the question over dinner and I thought he was kidding, but he got down on one knee and proposed," explains Jenny. Even more surprising than his marriage offer, though was the fact that her cat Rudy jumped up on the table hissing the moment he proposed. "He hopped right up there and started walking though his spaghetti," explains Jenny. "He never went on the table. Now he was out of control all of a sudden." Jenny was so very confused by everything. She really liked Ronnie and she didn't want to lose him, but it was so soon, and she just couldn't stop thinking about why her cat hated him so much.

Suddenly everything felt wrong for Jenny and her cat was going crazy. She politely told Ronnie that she couldn't possibly marry him right now and that they should get to be good friends first for at least another year or so. "He said he understood, but I could tell by his eyes he was angry about me saying no," remembers Jenny. "Then he stormed out of here saying he'd call me the next day." But Jenny never saw or heard from him ever again.

Ronnie was gone without a trace, and nobody knew his whereabouts. "I know I didn't know him that well, but it was still hard to take," admits Jenny. "I missed him, and he did break my heart." Jenny was hurt and sad, but she took it well. She reasoned that it was better he break her heart now rather than do more harm down the road.

But she didn't realize just how right she was until six months later when she was reading the local paper and there was Ronnie. He was wanted in three different states for marrying unsuspecting widows to con them out of their fortunes. "I was so shocked," says Jenny. "I couldn't move when I saw that newspaper article. All I kept thinking was if it wasn't for my cat, I may have not have been as careful as I was. He saved me! I made a decision then that Rudy was the only man I needed around the house for a while."

For the next three years Jenny kept things simple in her life, and Rudy was her main male. That was until she finally DID meet the man of her dreams. And with Rudy's glowing approval, they married. "He's never even once hissed at him," says Jenny of her new man. "And he loves Rudy as much as I do."

A Place to Put
Their Love

The situation was simple but serious for Helen and Arthur. Fifty-two-year-old Helen had limited upward mobility after narrowly escaping death a few years earlier and was restricted to a wheelchair. The epileptic woman lost her balance when she suffered a seizure while walking along a busy street and fell into oncoming traffic. Meanwhile, her forty-nine-year-old husband, Arthur, had a similarly challenging existence. He had been blind since birth.

Helen dealt with her infirmity as best as she could with Arthur's help. "I used to be very independent despite my illness," says Helen. "Now I had no choice but to depend heavily on others. It was difficult to adjust to." Unable to work any longer at her old job as an office manager at a mortgage company, she did bring in a small income as a part-time receptionist at the same company. It helped out with the insurance benefits, and kept up her spirits. "I hated the thought that I was some kind of burden," says Helen. "I wanted to contribute."

Helen met Arthur twenty-seven years earlier while they were attending community college in Oklahoma City and became his champion. She helped him pick himself up out of his self-pity and move out of his parents' house and start a life of his own. With her help he got a job as an information clerk with the county where he eventually worked himself up the ladder to become a supervisor. They got married two years later, and for the last twenty-five years they had lived in wedded bliss.

But since her accident Arthur needed to be her protector. And it wasn't easy since the medical bills mounted way beyond what the insurance paid. But the straw that finally broke the camel's back was when Arthur was laid off from his job because of cutbacks. "The bottom line is we were busted," reveals Arthur. "There was no money left. We were living on credit and the good grace of the bank, which wouldn't last much longer."

Six months behind on their mortgage and with no place to get more money, things looked bleak to say the least. Yet, they never stopped loving each other nor did they ever let the financial problems change their positive outlook on life. "Somehow we just knew we would be alright because we had each other," remembers Helen. "As long as we had that support we could overcome anything."

But no matter how much love they had, they couldn't prevent the bank from foreclosing on the home they had happily lived in for eighteen years. And so without any dependable and substantial income and only three days to pay the bank, they put an ad in the paper to sell all their belongings and prepared to move into a cheap motel. They both cried as they readied all of their prized possessions for sale but took comfort in each other. They were there for each other no matter what.

When the day of their sale arrived, they got dressed and tidied up their house wanting to put their best foot forward. As bargain hunters sifted through their memories and the life they had shared together looking for deals they both just smiled and said hello. "We were really hurting knowing that our lives were being taken away like that, piece by piece, but we hugged each other and helped each other through it," says Arthur. In fact, they were so visibly in love with each other that all those who attended their sale were overcome. One after another they commented on what an inspiring couple they were. With each compliment Arthur and Helen simply smiled and thanked them, never sharing their desperate and sad story. "We thought people had plenty of their own problems," says Helen. "Why would they want to hear about ours?"

But all of that changed when an older gentleman in a

wheelchair named Ron wheeled himself into their house and hearts with a story of his own to tell. "The second we met Ron, he said he was going to be our best friend, but we thought that was just talk," remembers Arthur. "When he started talking we were blown away." As Ron shared his remarkable past with the couple, they noticed how it bore a striking similarity to their own experiences.

Ron was born with muscular dystrophy and was totally dependent on his parents until he met Sarah, the woman of his dreams, when he was thirty years old. She gave him the love and courage he needed to make a life for himself and her together. They married and Ron overcame his obstacles to become a wealthy and respected manufacturer of sporting goods. "He joked that Sarah convinced him that if he couldn't 'Just Do It' like the TV ad said then he could get rich selling sports equipment to people who could," remembers Arthur. But then after thirty years together, Sarah was diagnosed with lung cancer. And now it was up to Ron to become her rock. For the next seven years he helped her fight that disease until she finally did beat it. Now the two were happily enjoying their retirement.

Upon hearing his extraordinary story Arthur and Helen felt compelled to share their tale of happiness and hardship with Ron. "We felt he would understand," says Helen. "And we wanted to open up to him after he shared his personal story with us."

When Ron heard their story he broke down crying, then

he hugged them both and told them that their love would see them through. Then he left rather unexpectedly without buying a thing. Helen and Arthur thought they had shared too much. "I'm so proud," admits Helen. "The first thing I thought was maybe we were just feeling sorry for ourselves, and that he didn't want to hear it."

The couple put Ron out of their thoughts and continued with their sale, successfully selling most of their items that weekend. They counted their blessings and their money figuring out that they had made enough to afford the next three or four months of rent at the hotel they were planning on moving into. Hopefully, by then Arthur would find another job and they could survive.

When Monday morning arrived they packed their few remaining personal items into their old Chevy station wagon and prepared to say a sad good-bye to their home for the last time. But just then a shiny, brand-new Cadillac pulled up into the driveway, and an unfamiliar older woman emerged from the driver's side. She walked up to Helen and Arthur with tears in her eyes and introduced herself as Sarah, Ron's wife, and she handed the couple an envelope. Inside was the mortgage to their house paid in full. Helen was in shock! "It all happened so fast I didn't even understand it when I read the paper for the first time," says Helen. "I thought that somebody else had bought the house and they were moving in. But then I looked at the name on the mortgage and it was clearly ours. They bought our house for us!" Barely able to contain herself long enough to explain the miraculous news to Arthur, Sarah helped fill in the blanks. Apparently when Ron had heard their story he was so moved by their love and support of each other that he wanted to help in whatever way he could. So he was giving them the house as a gift.

As soon as Arthur understood what had happened he threw his arms around Sarah. Then the couple both thanked Sarah over and over again swearing their lifelong love and friendship to her and her husband. When Helen insisted they would find a way to pay them back, Sarah told them exactly how they could deliver in full. "She only asked that we keep loving each other forever," says Arthur. "And that's has been one of the easiest promises I've ever had to keep."

A Sure Bet

*M*ichael should have been happy with his life. The tall, dark, and handsome investment analyst had a caring and concerned wife, a wonderful son, and a very well-paying career on Wall Street. But he never got over the pain of his father leaving home before he was born and then being abandoned by his alcoholic, gambling mother when he was just thirteen years old. "I felt it was my fault she left, like there was something wrong with me," admits Michael. "I was carrying that with me my whole life."

Michael was shifted from one foster home to another but never was adopted. Then he was finally set out into the world on his own when he was eighteen years old. He did well for himself on his own, working his way through college and graduating at the top of his class from UCLA, then snagging a great job as a junior analyst for one of New York's biggest brokerage houses. He shot up the ladder quickly, becoming a vice president by the time he was thirty-two years old. He met and married Diana, a nurse he was introduced to at a friend's party, and a few years later he was the proud father of a beautiful baby boy they named Lucas.

But even the love of his wife and child as well as the fruits of his labor couldn't rid Michael of the pains of his past. "It was never enough. I still felt worthless inside. I was someone that nobody wanted—not even my own mother. All the money in the world couldn't change that," reveals Michael. Michael tried everything to kill the pain, filling his life with expensive toys he didn't need and wining and dining his family and friends at the most expensive restaurants in town.

However nothing made him feel any better—in fact nothing made him feel. "As a child I learned to shut off my emotions to get through the rough times," says Michael. "But when I grew up and things were better I never learned how to truly turn my heart back on. So I never knew how to be happy."

Then one day while attending a meeting in Atlantic City, he walked into a casino and gambled for the first time in his life. "I felt so at home the moment I walked into that casino," admits Michael. "It was the strangest thing, but it made me feel alive." One sleepless night later he was hooked. He won a hundred bucks, but he gained a habit which would cost him everything.

A few short weeks later, Michael took Friday off from work and convinced his wife, Diana, to get a sitter for their now three-year-old-son, promising her a romantic weekend in Atlantic City. But just as soon as they checked in to the hotel, Michael was in the casino feeding his habit with total disregard of his wife. "Diana was so insulted and confused," says Michael. "She knew I never gambled before so she was shocked. She begged me to stop, but I just ignored her. I was so screwed up that she was completely invisible to me." Outside of dinners and one show plus a few hours sleep here and there, Michael spent the majority of the weekend in the casino frantically throwing his money away on everything from slot machines to craps and roulette. When he discovered blackjack he knew it was for him. "I probably lost a couple of grand at the tables that weekend," remembers Michael. "I lost so much money I actually became physically ill afterward just thinking about it. The fact that I wasn't eating or sleeping much made things worse. I felt like I was going to die."

Michael returned home with his wife after the nightmarish weekend wracked with guilt over what he had done. But it didn't stop him from continuing his gambling habit, returning to Atlantic City a few weeks later on his own to lose another bundle of cash. Finally, as their bank account began to dwindle, his wife forced him to promise he would never gamble again. "I agreed to make her feel better, but I knew there was no way I was going to give it up," says Michael. "I was way beyond being sensible about the whole thing. I was very sick and I needed serious help, but I didn't know it, and neither did she at that point."

Over the course of the next three years Michael raised the stakes of his habit however he could. He found out through friends about illegal gambling facilities all over Manhattan and was betting on everything from sports to political elections. If the bookies were placing odds on it he would bet on it. "Not a day went by that I didn't bet on something," reveals Michael. "I physically needed to gamble." It wasn't long before his work began to suffer. Soon he was ducking out of the office in the middle of the week claiming family emergencies and driving to Atlantic City. Telling his wife he had to work late, he'd gamble the night away losing far more than he ever won.

Just three years after starting his habit he had lost over fifty thousand dollars, and worse yet, he was running out of money to pay off his gambling debts. Soon he had to trade his possessions to keep his legal and illegal creditors happy. The first time he couldn't pay, he traded his ten-thousand-dollar Rolex watch to a bookie in exchange for erasing a $2,500 debt without even thinking twice about it. Incredibly, Michael was so addicted he made another bet with the same bookie just an hour later.

His gambling habit was now so extreme that his wife

threatened to leave him unless he got help, and his boss asked him to take off a month and work out whatever his problem was. But instead of working on his problem, he went on a gambling binge.

That month Michael lost a whopping sixty-two-thousand dollars—just about every penny he and his wife had in the bank. But he didn't stop there. He kept gambling the family right into a ten-grand hole. His wife found out how much trouble they were in when she tried to pay for her groceries and her debit card was denied for insufficient funds. "The crying was the worst," remembers Michael. "At that point nothing could get through to me though. Subconsciously, I suppose I believed I could never amount to anything better than my mother. So I proceeded to abandon my family, just like my mom had done to me."

Amazingly, Michael's devoted wife still didn't leave him, instead begging him to get help. But Michael decided he didn't need anyone—only his habit and himself. He moved out of the house and into a small apartment leaving his wife and child to fend for themselves. Now Diana was raising their six-year-old boy alone with little or no money coming from her gambling husband who had just walked out the door. She had no choice but to go back to work at her old job as a nurse to pay the bills. And though Michael reported back for work at the end of the month claiming he was fit as a fiddle, he couldn't have been sicker. And he was about to come face-to-face with the possibility of losing everything.

Over the next several months he fell deeper and deeper into the world of gambling. Finally, during one of his routine visits to a local illegal gaming joint, a police raid landed Michael in a precinct house with not a soul to post bail. "It was the lowest point in my life," remembers Michael. "I sat there trying to think of who I could call. There was nobody. I'd abandoned my family and friends, I couldn't call my boss and confess to him, and even my lawyer wasn't talking to me because of what I'd done to my wife." With not a soul to call and lacking the $1,000 cash needed to get out of jail, Michael spent the next several days behind bars.

Meanwhile, unaware of her husband's incarceration, Diana was about to face the greatest challenge of her life and Michael wouldn't be there to help. The same day he was arrested, she woke up to find her darling son covered in unexplainable bruises. She rushed him to the hospital where she was told the worst possible news—that he had leukemia and was dying! He needed a bone marrow transplant immediately, and Michael was the most likely donor. "I felt so alone at the time when I needed the most support," remembers Diana. "I wished and prayed so much that Michael was here with me. But I wasn't holding my breath." Diana tried to reach her husband at work but was told he never showed up. Despite what he had done to her, she was still devoted to him. Worried sick about what happened she called every hospital in town. Then she called the police to report him missing and discovered the shocking news that her husband was behind bars. "It was like the whole world was exploding," remembers Diana. "I needed my husband back now more than ever."

Diana immediately rushed to the city jail and bailed out her husband, hoping she could say something to him that would wake him up. Before Michael even had a chance to make up some lame excuse Diana blurted out the shocking news of their son's dilemma, stopping him dead in his tracks. "She said, 'Luke is dying of leukemia, and you're the only one that can save him. So I need you to get your act straight right now!' " recalls Michael. "It was like I got hit by a Mack truck. My whole body went limp and I started to cry." Michael was suddenly transported to a place in his heart that he never knew he had. The thought of somebody needing him so much somehow made him feel important and worthwhile. "Without a doubt the thought foremost in my head at that moment was 'I have to save my baby'," reveals Michael. "And as soon as I thought it, I realized I was different. As crazy as it sounds I suddenly knew I was capable of caring and somehow that made all the difference. I had changed."

As Diana waited in horrible suspense hoping the news would break through to her husband but fearing it wouldn't, Michael threw his arms around his wife and begged her for forgiveness. "He just kept saying 'I'm sorry' over and over again," says Diana. "Then he told me he loved me. Something was definitely different inside of him."

Diana paid the bail money, and Michael spent the next two days at the hospital where he and his son underwent a series of tests and procedures. The first victory came when doctors confirmed Michael was a perfect donor for his son. Then came the endless tests to see if his son could survive the transplant and the possible rejection. But after all was said and done, the procedure was a go.

Michael approached his boss to ask for more time off, but first he confessed he had a gambling addiction and was going to get help. "I thought he was going to fire me," explains Michael. "But it turns out he was a recovering alcoholic and he helped me get into a program."

Michael checked into the hospital right before Christmas to try and save his son's life. After enduring the painful process of having his marrow removed, he watched his life's blood pump into his son while his wife held their child in her arms. "When I saw that, all at once it became clear how important I was to these two very special and beautiful people," reveals Michael. "They needed me and I needed to get the help that would enable me to be there for them." Two days later they found out that the operation was a complete success.

Lucas came home a month later and Michael enrolled

in a treatment program for gamblers that week. He stopped gambling and hasn't been within a hundred feet of a wager in over ten years. Meanwhile the couple has been blessed with three more children, and both Michael and his wife have become tireless advocates who fight to raise awareness of children's diseases. "The only thing I'll ever bet on again is the love of my family," says Michael. "And that's a bet I can't lose."

Daddy's Little Love

When Rosalind was a little girl she was always hopping up on her father's big, strong lap whenever she could. As she grew up, he was still always there to teach, to love, and to help. But when Rosalind was a teenager, the longtime hard-living sailor was diagnosed with a critical heart condition. There was no avoiding the cold, hard truth that he was dying, and all Rosalind wanted to do was save his life. "I didn't want my daddy to die," remembers Rosalind. "Mom and I were close, too, but my dad was like my special pal."

Her father was everything to Rosalind. He always had a way of finding the time to spend hours every weekend with her on her favorite hobby—building model airplanes. And her father loved teaching her about his favorite hobby, cooking. No matter what it was, from dating to donning a new dress, if it had to do with Rosalind, her father was interested. "He was really different than other dads," recalls Rosalind. "I could talk to him about anything—even girl stuff. On the outside he was this rough and gruff sailor but underneath all that he was a real pussycat."

But almost overnight, Rosalind's dad's health deteriorated and her gentle giant wound up in the hospital with a grim prognosis. Years of hard living and hard drinking had taken its toll on the crusty sailor's system and now just about everything was malfunctioning. "He was dying and there was nothing that I could do," explains Rosalind. "I felt so helpless and scared. I didn't want to lose my dad." Rosalind broke down, crying like a baby to her dad, begging him not to leave her. Her loving father just held her tightly and told her he loved her and always would. "I don't want to die either," he said to his beloved daughter. "But we all have to go sometime." The words weren't much of a comfort to Rosalind, though. As she struggled to come to terms with the inevitable, her father's condition continued to decline. Then one day as Rosalind walked into her father's hospital room to visit, she was shocked to see doctors trying to resuscitate him. He'd gone into cardiac arrest.

The doctors worked hard to save him, but it was too late. Her father died in front of her and she didn't even get a chance to say goodbye. It was a tragedy she could not get past. "I knew I wasn't ready to see him go, but for him to die in front of my eyes was just too much, and I kept thinking that if I had arrived a few minutes earlier maybe I could have saved him or done something. I thought about that over and over again," admits Rosalind.

Rosalind would carry that painful thought with her for years to come—was there something that she could have done? She was so obsessed by the thought that she could have saved her dad that it inspired her to learn CPR years later. In some unexplainable way it made her feel better. "I knew it would never bring Dad back," explains Rosalind. "But at least I knew that if I had to, I really could save someone else's life."

Soon after taking her CPR class, Rosalind and her mother went to Reno on a weekend trip. At the end of the stormy weekend—after canceling two return flights out of Reno because of her mother's fear of flying in bad weather—Rosalind and her mom set out to head back to California on a third flight once the skies cleared. As they arrived at the airport and walked toward their gate, Rosalind was reminded of her dying father in a most extraordinary way.

Suddenly just a few feet in front of her an older man collapsed to the floor. He was having a heart attack, and amazingly as she glanced at the man's face she thought she saw her father. "He was the spitting image of him," says Rosalind. "I was frozen. I couldn't believe it. His hair, his face, his build it was so much like my dad." While Rosalind stood stunned, others tried to assist him but several passersby walked right on by the dying man doing nothing to help. Then she heard someone yell out that his heart had stopped, and Rosalind knew exactly what she had to do. "I knew this was my dad sending me a message. He was giving me a chance to get rid of the pain and the guilt I was carrying for all these years. It was my dad taking care of me just like he used to. But first I had to take care of someone else and save a life," remembers Rosalind.

She rushed over to the man and knelt by his side, noting even more how closely he resembled her father. She felt for a pulse, but there was none. She screamed for someone to call for an ambulance. "I thought about how this man could have a daughter or a son, and I had to save him so I could prevent them from going through what I had endured," remembers Rosalind. "I knew there was no time to wait for an ambulance. I was his only hope. If I didn't do something he was going to die." Rosalind went to work. She pounded on the man's chest. Then she pressed her lips against his and began mouth-to-mouth resuscitation. But she needed to have someone help—she couldn't do both at the same time. She spied a burly security guard around the corner and summoned him over to help out by pounding on the portly man's chest. As Rosalind puffed away, she instructed the guard to push harder and faster on the man's chest. "I was determined to save his life," says Rosalind.

"My father's death made me realize just how important life is and how important fathers are. This man was more than just my dad now—he was every dad. I loved this man and his family even though I didn't know them. I had to save him." Tears streamed down Rosalind's face as she fought to save his life. And then finally, as if it were a gift from above, his chest rose and he took a breath.

Almost instantly his eyes opened to meet Rosalind's. He was alive! "It was the greatest feeling I ever had in my whole life when I looked into those eyes. My dad was alive again in my heart. I knew the man was going to be alright, and I knew I was going to be too," says Rosalind. The man stared silently into Rosalind's eyes as he took his first breaths. Somehow they knew each other; they understood each other. Before any words could be spoken paramedics arrived to rush the stranger to the local hospital where he was treated for a massive heart attack. Rosalind had saved his life. They exchanged silent smiles as he was carted away. Then Rosalind and her mother boarded their plane back to California.

The next day she received a phone call from a man named David, the son of the man whose life she had saved. The older man's name was Bob. He was a state assembly-man from Las Vegas, and David thanked her from the bottom of his heart for saving his father's life. "I told him I was grateful for the opportunity to help," says Rosalind.

"Little did he know just how true that was." David invited Rosalind back to Las Vegas to visit with his father who wanted to thank her personally. Rosalind accepted the invitation.

The next day she walked into the hospital in Las Vegas ready to meet the man whose life she saved and who changed her life. "A flood of memories rushed through my heart as I walked into his hospital room," explains Rosalind. "Everything was just like when I visited my dad the day he died—all the smells and the sounds were exactly the same and I started to shake." As Rosalind walked into the room, she was again flabbergasted at how much this man looked like her father. "Special delivery for Bob," she said cheerfully as she handed him over a little gumball machine and some M&Ms. Bob called in his wife, Nancy, and his son and daughter and Bob wrapped his arms around Rosalind like only a father could as they all embraced Rosalind as a new part of their family.

Since then Rosalind's look-alike dad has become an important part of her life, always just a phone call away when she needs a pick-me-up or just a "special pal" to talk with. "I can never replace dear old dad, but every time I talk to Bob it feels like my dad never left," says Rosalind.

Hearts on Fire

$\mathcal{V}$ ince was a hero. As a captain on St. Louis's famed Fire and Rescue Squad #2, he had saved countless lives throughout his thirty-one-year career as a rescue fireman by getting people safely out of deadly situations while risking his own life along the way. But his desire to help didn't end there. When he was finished saving lives, he went to work making life a little easier for many as chief of the St. Louis Salvation Army's Disaster Service. Vince loved helping people because he believed it was the right way to live, and that's because some very special people taught him to live that way by their own beautiful and caring example.

Vince grew up during the fifties on the mean inner city streets of St. Louis, and life wasn't easy for the young African American boy from a hard-working but poor family. His father worked two jobs so he could pay the bills and send his son to private school so he'd have a better chance of getting out of the ghetto. "My dad busted his backside so we'd always have food on the table, but everything else was pretty tough. My parents had to make great sacrifices to put me in that private school, but they were devoted to giving me every opportunity to make something out of my life," remembers Vince.

But even in spite of Vince's parents' attempts to keep him on the straight and narrow and on the road to success, he was headed for trouble, stealing and skipping school until an unlikely bunch of firefighters from the station house behind his school came to the rescue. Young Vince had wanted to be a firefighter from the time he was a little boy. He loved the bells and whistles and the way they always saved the day. So when the firefighters saw Vince poking around the station and asked him to be the firehouse runner, it was a dream come true. "I practically lived at that firehouse, and they whipped me into shape," says Vince. Despite the racial barriers at the time, the all-white fire crew took Vince under their wing, and made sure he was on the right track. They helped him with his homework, made sure he was going to school and when they found out he was getting into trouble, they laid down the law. "I used to have this bad habit as kid of stealing donuts," reveals Vince. "But when they heard I was doing that they called a couple of their police officer friends in and gave me a good scare that snapped me right out of that fast. They really loved me."

Vince's parents' love and devotion plus the friendship of the firemen paid off. Vince graduated high school with honors and received a football scholarship to college. The model student was at the top of his class in 1962 when he saw an ad for the army and signed up to support his country's calling to fight the war in Vietnam as a Green Beret.

But three years later, Vince returned not to cheers but jeers and insults. As Vince fought to put his life back together and find himself, the firehouse saved him once again. This time he became a fireman. "It was my childhood dream," says Vince. "And making it a reality saved my life. I knew it was what I was meant to do."

Vince was a natural lifesaver. His strong, towering six-feet-two-inch rock-solid build and his heart of gold and unrelenting desire to go above and beyond the call of duty to help others made him into a model rescue fireman. He was promoted from private to captain in two short years, and his unconventional methods and never-say-die attitude quickly earned him a reputation for being a no-nonsense guy who didn't accept defeat. "He was real tough on the outside but pure heart on the inside," says Lucky, one of his fellow captains. "The bottom line is that he cared about people, and he never gave up on them." Tackling a man off a scaffold ten stories up to prevent him committing suicide was just one example of how Vince was devoted to helping at all costs. There were countless other heroic moments.

But being a great rescue fireman wasn't enough for Vince. He wanted to do more. After being comforted by a Salvation Army Disaster worker who warmed him up with a cup of coffee and bowl of chili on a cold winter's night while he was fighting to save lives, Vince decided he would join up. In no time at all he took on the awesome responsibility of being a chief for the relief organization, which often found him caring for his fellow firemen. "We all really respected Vince a great deal," says Lucky. "Most fireman do some kind of volunteer work on their time off, but he went all the way. He was totally dedicated to helping others, including so many of us. When we were tired and fatigued at a fire, there was Vince with his Salvation Army truck ready to help. We all really appreciated him for that. He was always a colleague and a friend to all of us."

Deep-caring Vince often went right from his shifts as a fire captain to his Salvation Army duties. On one particular June night after Vince helped to battle an eight-alarm magnesium fire through the night, he drove home and changed into his Salvation Army uniform then headed right back out to the fire to fight the next good fight, giving comfort to the next shift of fireman battling the blaze. Vince stayed until the firefighters were called off, handing out coffee, snacks, and kind words to keep them all going.

When the night's work was done Vince and the firemen packed up and headed for home, only Vince didn't make it that far. A heart attack stopped him dead in his tracks. "I felt fine and then all of a sudden my chest tightened up," recalls Vince. "Then everything went black." Vince suffered a massive heart attack, and as he fell unconscious his Salvation Army truck swerved into the curb and came to a halt.

Now Vince's life was out of his hands, but a lifetime of loving others was about to pay off. Just moments after Vince collapsed, the very same firefighters he had been comforting for hours came driving by, including his pal Lucky. When they saw Vince's truck up on the curb they knew something was very wrong, but they had no idea just how serious the situation was. "We pulled up alongside the truck and we saw him passed out in the driver's seat," recalls Lucky. "We rushed over to help him and he was dead, there was no question about it!" Vince was without a pulse or a heartbeat and he wasn't breathing. As the firefighters worked feverishly to save the man who had devoted his life to saving others, Lucky spotted the paramedics also on their way back from the fire turning the corner and quickly flagged them down. Without a moment to lose the medical crew performed emergency CPR and jumpstarted his heart with a defibrillator. His heart started to beat again. But seconds later it stopped. Paramedics kept frantically defibrillating him finally bringing Vince back to life again. "It really was touch-and-go there for a few minutes," says Lucky. "But I knew we were going to save him. We had to, we just plain had to." Lucky immediately ordered the ambulance to rush his friend to the nearest hospital. Just a few short minutes later Vince was safe and sound in the hospital intensive care unit talking up a storm and asking for his friends. "He was amazing," says Lucky. "The guy had just died and here he was asking about us. He's a hell of a guy."

A week later Vince was out of the hospital and back on his feet but not before learning from doctors that if he hadn't been where he was that night helping out with the Salvation Army, he surely would have died. "Lucky saved my life," says Vince. "And I can never truly repay him for that. So I guess all I can do to make good on that help is to keep on helping others."

Anything for Love

⁓

*K*ip was just seven years old when his father deserted him and his mom, Shirley, leaving him wondering what he did wrong to chase his father away. But his loving mother bore the brunt of the storm for her young son. She buried her own pain so she could assure him that nothing bad was going to happen to him. She swore she'd protect him and love him for the rest of her life. "Right after my father left she sat me down and put her arms around me and promised me that she would never leave me no matter what," reveals Kip. "She told me she'd be a mom and a dad to me." That promise of love and support is what kept Kip going for the rest of his childhood.

Shirley worked hard to make sure Kip grew up with all

the opportunities that other children with two parents had even though it meant working night and day and hardly ever sleeping. "I wanted him to feel safe, so I worked very long hours so we would have financial security," says Shirley. "But I also needed him to feel like he had a mom there when he came home from school." The Detroit, Michigan, single and caring mom worked two jobs—one as a waitress on the day shift at a local restaurant and the other as a registered nurse on the graveyard shift from eleven to five A.M. six days a week at a local hospital. Her schedule was hectic to say the least.

On an average day, Shirley would take Kip to school at eight A.M. then head off to sling hash until quitting time at two P.M., early enough to pick up Kip from school at three. Then everyday after school mother and son sat down and talked about the day. Then Shirley would cook dinner, grab four hours of sleep, wake up and put her child to bed and head off to work at the hospital. Shortly after her husband left she invited her single sister to live with them so there would be someone in the house while Kip slept. The supermom kept that routine up until Kip was eighteen years old. "The schedule was really killing me at first," admits Shirley. "I was so exhausted. But after awhile you get used to it. You learn the value of catnaps, especially when you know someone you love is depending on you."

Her unusual schedule allowed her to secure a good living for her and her son while still being able to be there for him and spend quality time with him everyday. "I didn't want him to be a latchkey kid," explains Shirley. "I saw how those kids got into so much trouble coming into the hospital with drug overdoses and all kinds of problems even when they had two parents. With just me I knew he needed all the attention I could give him."

Shirley did her best to stay true to her promise to be both a mom and dad to her son. When he complained to her that he wasn't big and strong enough to hit home runs in baseball, Shirley taught him how to successfully throw a killer curveball, sure to strike out the bigger kids. "I still don't know how she ever learned how to do that," says Kip. "But she made me feel like a real star." But Shirley also taught young Kip how to cook a killer lasagna and how to sew on a button if he should ever need to. She also checked his homework every day, made him breakfast, lunch and dinner, read to him before tucking him in and leaving for work, and spent at least an hour each day just sharing their time, and thoughts together. "I made a mistake when I married my husband and I knew that, but he gave me a beautiful son, and I wasn't going to foul that up, no matter what," explains Shirley. Kip was ecstatic the day he made his middle school baseball team, but not half as proud as Shirley. "I felt so alone the first time I went to watch him play—it seemed like I was the only parent there alone," remembers Shirley. "But as soon as I saw him in his bright little uniform take the field and wave to me, I was the happiest woman on earth." And when Kip made the honor roll in high school, there was mom again feeling like the proudest parent on earth. And, finally, when Kip won an academic and athletic scholarship to Northwestern University, and graduated high school with honors, he thanked his mom in his yearbook promising he'd always be there for her. "I always worried whether or not I was doing things right when he was growing up," remembers Shirley. "But when I saw him graduate and I read those words in the yearbook, I knew for sure I did a good job with Kip."

That summer after graduation Kip readied himself to leave Detroit for his first semester at Northwestern. Shirley quit her waitressing job in June so she and her son could spend even more time with each other during the summer before he went off to school.

Then just weeks before Kip was ready to leave for school, he woke up one morning and noticed that his mother hadn't returned home from her graveyard shift at the hospital. He was worried. In all the years she had had the job she was never late returning home in the morning. "That wasn't like her at all," says Kip. "I knew something had to be wrong." Just as Kip prepared to call the hospital and check on his mom, the phone rang. It was the hospital—his mother had been in a head-on collision. Kip jumped in his car and rushed down to the emergency room where he was met by the doctor who told him of his mother's grim diagnosis. She'd been hit head-on by a drunk driver and the impact crushed her tailbone. Doctors said she was paralyzed and would never walk again. When Kip walked in to see her he didn't even recognize her. "She was covered from head to toe in bandages and tubes," remembers Kip. "And she was so sad. I hadn't seen her that depressed since my dad left. I wanted to help her but I didn't know what to do."

Meanwhile, all Shirley was thinking of was her loving son. The moment she saw his face she started crying and apologizing to him for making a mess of things right before he left for college. "I couldn't believe that she was feeling bad for *me!*" remembers Kip. "I was supposed to be sorry for her. I put my hands on her lips and stopped her right away. I told her I loved her, and I was there for her no matter what just like she had said to me when I was a kid. It made her smile."

When the doctors told Shirley and son the prognosis, they both cried and held each other. Then when the doctor spoke of the need for a full-time nurse or someone at home while she recuperated, Kip immediately assured the doctor and his mother he would be there. His mother looked at him in shock. "I told her I wasn't going to go off to college and desert her," explains Kip. "We actually got into an argument in front of the doctor because she didn't want me to stay and miss out on my scholarship." The last thing that devoted mom Shirley wanted was for her son to sacrifice his schooling for her, so she protested vehemently.

But when he insisted with tears in his eyes she finally understood. "I didn't want this to stand in the way of his success, but all he wanted to do was help me," says Shirley. "I knew I couldn't talk him out of it."

And Shirley was right. That fall Shirley came home from the hospital in a wheelchair. Kip enrolled in night classes at a local community college and took a job working at the same restaurant his mom had worked at. Suddenly it was as if the roles were reversed. Kip worked the lunch shift so he could be there for his mom at night after she returned from her rehabilitation at the hospital. He cooked three meals a day for her and took catnaps while attending classes at night and studying into the wee hours of the morning. For the next six years, Kip's number one goal was to help her heal. "The doctors said they had little hope that she would ever be able to use her legs again," says Kip. "But they did say there was a chance that maybe she could have some movement. I was determined to try everything to see her walk again." He spent just about every free moment taking care of his mom and helping her with the rehabilitation, feeding her and keeping her spirits up. He took her out to movies, talked with her about her thoughts and fears, and was her best friend just like she was with him for so many years.

As the years passed Kip slowly progressed in his studies finally deciding on physical therapy because of his mom's plight, and the more he learned the more he could help his mom. "Caring for her made me more sympathetic to all the people out there who needed that kind of help," says Kip. "So I suddenly knew how I wanted to dedicate my life."

As doctors worked out the details of long-term care for Shirley, Kip was helping her plan pleasure cruises around the world for after she recovered. "I knew that she would walk again—I could see it in her eyes," remembers Kip. "She had the will and the strength to make it happen. She just needed someone to believe in her and help her through. I was going to be that person." From his studies Kip knew the body inside out and understood that the type of damage his mother experienced had been healed before. He knew with nutrition, rehabilitation and lots of love anything was possible. And he never stopped believing.

Then one day Shirley started complaining about a strange pain in her back. It worried and concerned Kip. The next day when he walked into her room she was standing balancing herself by holding on to the dresser. "I was stunned," admits Kip. "I knew it could happen, but for it to happen like that was beyond explanation." But while doctors fumbled for some precise medical explanation, they confirmed that the power of Kip's support was instrumental in her standing. "It was not impossible for her to walk again one day but for it to happen as quickly as it did was certainly against any medical odds," says one doctor. "There was obviously something beyond medicine going on here, and I believe it was the power of love."

Within a few weeks of her amazing recovery Shirley was out of her wheelchair for good relying only on her walker, but it wasn't long before that, too, was only a memory. "I just felt so strong all of a sudden," recalls Shirley. "And I know it was because of Kip's support. He was always there for me." Amazingly only a year later, Shirley was walking well enough to start back to work at her old job in the hospital part time. And six years after being told she might never walk again she was back working full-time.

Confident that his mom was back on her feet, Kip finally finished his education and pursued the dream his mother's injury inspired—to become a certified physical therapist. Eventually he even started his own successful practice where mom Shirley helped out two days a week to help keep the expenses low. Things were going well for mother and son again. They had overcome two tragedies in life, but incredibly their greatest challenge was yet to come.

Kip's business was booming, and he was getting ready to marry, settle down, and make Shirley a grandma when one day disaster struck in the form of a simple cramp. As Kip was eating breakfast he fell to the floor wracked with sharp, shooting abdominal pain. Fearful the pain could be caused by appendicitis, Kip's fiancée called 911, then called Shirley. Kip was rushed to the nearby hospital where they all learned the terrifying diagnosis—double kidney failure. Diabetes had been silently and slowly ravaging Kip's body for years but never affecting him badly enough for him to notice and something triggered his system now to react violently. If he didn't have a transplant immediately he would die. "It was terrifying," remembers Shirley. "He never had any medical problems his whole life. Then they tell me he is going to die. It was just too much. But I knew I had to be strong for him. Nothing was going to kill my son after all we'd been through."

While Kip lingered in his hospital bed in pain and confusion over how and why this happened, Shirley flew into action. Being a nurse she knew how long it could take to find a donor even in desperate circumstances, but she knew that there was a good chance that she was a match—and if she was she could save her son's life. "I knew it wasn't a sure thing," says Shirley. "We would have to be tested, but if I was a match we needed to find out quick." As mother and son waited anxiously for the results of the tests, they talked just like they did when he was a little boy crying because his dad left, just like they did when she was overcoming her crippling injury, and now once again as a team, mother and son fighting for survival with love as their greatest asset. Then the doctor walked in with the results. They were a match—a perfect match. "I threw my arms around my baby and hugged him so tight," says Shirley. "He just cried and told me how much he loved me."

Yet Kip, ever thoughtful, still wasn't ready to accept his mother's lifesaving gift until he made sure it was what she really wanted. "Can you believe he even thought to ask if I was sure it was alright with me?" says Shirley. "Here he was dying, asking me if I minded helping him. He's so sweet! I told him I would give both my kidneys if I needed to save him."

Less than a week later the transplant was done, and a month later Kip was back on his feet with a bright future ahead of him. Three years later Kip has had zero rejection of the perfect kidney his mom had donated. His physical therapy practice is thriving and he finally did settle down with his wife who blessed him with twin boys. But most of all he made his mom as proud a mom as there ever was. "When you see him with his wife and those little boys I know that all that love I gave my son went to good use," says new grandma Shirley. "Technically I may have given him a kidney, but what I really am proud of is giving him a heart."

Down on His Love

*P*atrick was homeless and thought he was completely helpless to ever change his life. The
twenty-eight-year old alcoholic vagrant was living on the
streets of Miami in the summer of 1997, barely surviving
on whatever he could scrape together from handouts. And
Patrick was ready to give up on trying. He was in bad shape
and he had no idea how it all had ever come to this.

Just three years earlier he was a happy and healthy young
man working as an up-and-coming chef in Las Vegas while
living with his loving and wealthy parents in their sprawling
palatial estate outside of the city. "I loved my family so
much—not because they were rich but because we were so
close, especially me and my dad," says Patrick. "Sometimes

we used to just sit up late at night when I'd get home from the restaurant and talk straight through till morning."

Life was sweet and meaningful for Patrick. He was slowly becoming respected in the business around town as one of the city's most promising chefs. His father was considering opening up a restaurant for him, and the future couldn't have looked any brighter.

But one day while taking his morning walk Patrick's father suddenly collapsed from a massive embolism in his brain. "My mom flipped out when it happened," remembers Patrick. His father died instantaneously. Patrick and his mother were beside themselves with grief. "She and my father met when they were six years old and grew up together. He was the only man she ever kissed and when she lost him she just went to pieces."

Patrick tried to be there as best as he could for his mother to comfort and love her, but no matter how he tried to help her, she just gradually drifted deeper and deeper into depression, and soon her depression turned to anger. "She started to blame me for what happened to my dad," explains Patrick "She wasn't in her right mind, but at the time I took it to heart. I had already lost my father, and now I felt I was losing my mother's love, too." His mother needed someone to lash out against for what had happened and Michael was the only one around.

His mother's troubles only worsened when she started drinking heavily, and she soon fell into a lifestyle of staying out late and sleeping all day. She became so distant with her son, Patrick, he hardly ever spoke to his mother anymore even though they were living in the same house. "She acted as if she wanted nothing to do with me, and when I tried to get through to her she got violent," recalls Patrick. "She'd start screaming and wind up throwing a plate or something at me."

To make matters worse she was meeting all the wrong kinds of people in her wayward lifestyle and taking comfort in the pretended kindness of manipulative and abusive men who were obviously only after her for her money. Patrick was beginning to feel like a stranger in his own mother's house. But most important he was worried sick over his mom and what she was doing to herself. Desperate to help her, Patrick finally told his departed father's lawyer what was happening, hoping he could help her since he was the executor of his dad's estate. One day pretending to have legal papers for her to sign, they asked her to come into the office where a psychiatrist, masquerading as a lawyer, was waiting to speak with her. But when the gentleman simply asked her if she was having difficulty getting over her husband's death, she flew out of the office in a rage.

Tragically, the next day Patrick returned home to find the locks changed on the doors and a note next to Patrick's packed suitcases outside the door. The note simply read, LEAVE! "I died when I read that note," remembers Patrick. "Everything I knew my life to be was over at that moment.

I loved my parents more than life itself. And now they were gone. Most of all I couldn't help my mom." Then as if matters couldn't get any worse, police showed up and arrested him. In her deranged state, she accused him of having beaten her. The charges were wholly untrue and eventually dropped, but not until Patrick languished in a jail cell for almost twenty-four hours. In his already fragile state the shock of what his mother did broke him. "That's when something snapped," remembers Patrick. "I just fell apart. I felt like I was all alone in the world with nowhere to turn. I thought my own mother hated me. After that I just stopped caring anymore about anything."

Patrick doesn't remember much about those next few months other than getting on a bus with $1,000 and some clothes and leaving town headed for nowhere in particular. The next two years of his life were a big blur of names and faces along the way. He eventually wound up at the end of the road, Miami, Florida. There he took one odd job after another but failed at each one, never able to truly focus on anything other than the hurt, pain, and confusion of what had happened. "I was trapped in the past," remembers Patrick. "I might have looked like I was present and accounted for on the outside, but I was gone on the inside. I just couldn't snap out of the hurt." Ironically, Patrick soon began drinking to kill the pain just like his mother had, and soon any hope for getting his life back together seemed lost forever. He quickly became a destitute alcoholic, and at twenty-eight-years old Patrick's greatest aspiration was to die. "I'm ashamed to say I prayed to God almost every night to let me get hit by a truck or shot," admits Patrick "I drank until I blacked out and that was the closest I could get to feeling dead. That was the only time I didn't feel the pain." Soon Patrick's life was reduced to wandering the streets in his now-tattered clothes and shoeless feet trying to get a buck or two to buy a beer, always claiming he needed the money for food.

But one day a thoughtful stranger insisted on giving Patrick a little more than he wanted. When Patrick pressed him for a dollar, he insisted on taking him for dinner instead. "I didn't want food," reveals Patrick. "I only ate about once every three days or so. All I wanted was a beer, and when he kept insisting on feeding me I told him so." When Patrick came clean with the thoughtful passerby, the stranger put his arm around Patrick and assured him he would help. "I was shocked," remembers Patrick. "Nobody even wanted to touch me let alone hug me when I was on the street. It made me feel human again." He convinced Patrick to tell him what led him to his downfall while he treated him to dinner.

After sharing his sad story, the helpful stranger surprised Patrick by taking out a piece of paper and beginning a business plan for how Patrick could get his life back together. In very factual and financial terms, he explained how Patrick's mother's condition was just like a company losing consumer confidence then taking a bad hit on the stock market. After confusing Patrick with a barrage of business terms, he stated simply that he had to get back to his mom and get his family back on track. "He sounded nuts at first," says Patrick. "But the more I started to listen, he started to make sense." Meanwhile all the business talk was making Patrick feel more like a professional and less like a bum. Finally, he told Patrick the number one reason why he needed to contact his mother. "He said me and my mother needed each other and families belonged together," says Patrick. "That hit me because I never stopped loving her." Then the stranger rose from the table and walked Patrick to a nearby pay phone and asked Patrick if he remembered his mother's number. Beaten Patrick nodded yes. The stranger dialed his calling access code into the phone then handed the receiver to Patrick to dial his mother's number. Patrick nervously dialed the number he could never forget and waited. "I didn't know if the number would even still be good," says Patrick. "Sadly, I didn't even know if she was alive or dead."

Three rings seemed like an eternity and then there she was. His mother answered. Patrick couldn't believe his ears. The voice sounded so sweet—like he remembered it sounding when he was a child, not like the angry, enraged woman who threw him out. Patrick was so nervous he couldn't speak. The stranger had to practically hold him up he was so weak with joy and apprehension. Finally Patrick summoned the courage to speak. "Mom—it's Patrick," he said fighting back the tears. "It's your son." But all Patrick heard was silence. Then finally the silence was broken, and Patrick heard the words he never thought he would ever hear again from his mom. "Patrick—I love you," said his mother softly, "I'm so sorry. Are you OK? Where are you? Please come home. I have been looking for you for so long." His mother rambled on, but Patrick couldn't hear anything after that. He just broke down crying hysterically while the stranger held him.

Patrick told his mother where he was and she arranged a ticket for him to fly home. The stranger rented a hotel room for Patrick to get cleaned up in and bought him a new outfit for the flight. Then late that night he drove him to the airport. "I told him I could never possibly repay him for what he did for me, but he wanted nothing, except he told me to just love my mom, and I promised him I would," says Patrick.

The next day Patrick was at home embracing his sorrowful mother. With her help he revived his cooking career. And now the two of them devote themselves to helping addicts kick their habits with an endowment started in the name of Patrick's father. And as Patrick's mom gets on in years, she knows her devoted son is there for her. "I've kept my promise to that stranger every day of my life," says Patrick proudly. "I love my mom with all my heart."

Something Borrowed

A s Emily enjoyed a delicious lunch with her husband of a few hours in a swank Seattle Italian restaurant, she just kept thinking about how much she had to be thankful for, especially after being in such a mess just a few years earlier. The twenty-seven-year-old woman had just married the man of her dreams and moved to Seattle from Atlanta to be with him. And her life was finally as she always wanted it to be. "It was like all my childhood dreams had come true," says Emily. "To think just a few years earlier my life was falling apart."

Three years before, Emily had just moved from the cozy confines of Montgomery, Alabama, to the big city of Atlanta in search of a career after graduating college. The small-town gal was scared and alone in the metropolis except for one friend who she knew from back home. Ironically, the two friends wound up living in the same apartment complex without even knowing it. "I just looked for the place with the best price," says Emily. "Then I was going to look him up once I got settled." When Emily called her friend Roz she found him living not only in the same complex but even in the same building.

She took a job as a customer service representative with long hours and little pay and struggled to make ends meet. Lonely and unaccustomed to the hustle and bustle of the city, she decided after the first several weeks that a drive back to Alabama for a pick-me-up was just what she needed. After packing her car with her luggage and her purse, she ran back into her apartment for a few forgotten items. When she returned she watched in horror as her money and most of her belongings drove away while her car was stolen right in front of her yes. "He was laughing at me as he drove by," remembers Emily. "I will never be able to forget how I felt. I was trying so hard to fight for survival, and that took everything out of me. I was ready to just give up and move right back to Alabama."

To make matters worse, Emily didn't have any insurance on the newly purchased car, and she was still making payments on it. Devastated, Emily called the police. And as she cried her eyes out in front of her apartment complex, a kind and thoughtful Roz found her and gave her a shoulder to cry on. "He just wanted to help in whatever way he could," remembers Emily. "And he didn't want anything—just to help. He's the only reason I didn't give up." Roz immediately offered to be her personal chauffeur whenever she needed. Everyday he came over and gave her a pick-me-up talk. He loaned her money for rent, groceries, and whatever else she needed, rarely asking to be repaid. "He was an absolute angel and he gave me the courage to stick it out," says Emily.

But despite her friend's help, the road ahead was still hard for Emily. Now even deeper in the hole than when she started out, Emily took a second job as a cocktail waitress working three or four nights a week till the wee hours of the morning just to make ends meet. Then she rose early in the morning to go to her other job. It wasn't long before the tough and tiring regimen finally took its toll on the young woman. One day as she rose to go to work with the flu and a raging fever, she stopped by Roz's apartment to say goodbye and she collapsed. "I was completely shot," says Emily. "I didn't even know where I was anymore. I was so sick and run-down, but I couldn't afford to stop working, so I just kept pushing myself until I lost it." Roz rushed her to the emergency room of the nearby hospital. Doctors determined she was suffering from exhaustion as well as the flu. They told her she needed to rest and Roz was there to make sure she did, running errands to buy groceries, medicines, or anything she needed to get herself back on her feet. "He took care of me," remembers Emily.

"Anything I needed he made sure I had. He really was my savior."

With Roz's help Emily got back on her feet and eventually found a better paying job which allowed her to quit her night job. Then, remarkably, almost two years after her car was stolen, police actually recovered it. It had been through the mill but her friend Roz helped her fix it up and sell it. "It was unbelievable how everything in my life was turning around," says Emily. "I was happy to be alive." Later that year Emily met Ray and fell in love—with Roz's approval of course. Suddenly life was looking real good for Emily. She moved to Seattle a few months later to be with Ray, and soon after that they became husband and wife.

Now, as Emily sat counting her blessings in the restaurant she couldn't help but think of what a difference it made in her life that somebody helped her when she was down. Just then Emily heard a commotion coming from the front of the restaurant. A woman was crying hysterically. Only moments later the owner walked in and told Emily that there was a woman outside who just suffered a terrible tragedy and he thought maybe she could help console her. It was a bride-to-be who was ready to tie the knot that night. And incredibly just hours before the most important night of her life, her car was stolen with her wedding dress, shoes, purse and everything she needed to make that night magical still inside. "I simply couldn't believe this was happening," says Emily. "I was just sitting there thinking about how Roz helped me when I had my car stolen and here's this woman. I knew I had to help her." Emily hurried toward the front of the restaurant to meet Amy, the twenty-five-year-old bride-to-be who had just had her dreams stomped on a by a thoughtless thief. "The owner told me to wait for help," says Amy. "I didn't really know what he could possibly do to help me, but I was so shook up I didn't know what I was doing. I stood there waiting in shock. I started thinking I wasn't going to be able to get married. It was horrible."

Just then Emily walked out and gave Amy a big hug and told her she was there to help. She took her by the hand and walked her into the other room where her beautiful wedding dress was draped over a chair where she had left it after changing a few hours earlier. Emily informed her that the dress was hers for the night. Amy was flabbergasted. "It was like she was my fairy godmother or something," says Amy. "I didn't waste any time telling her thank you and giving her a big hug. She saved my wedding." Only minutes later Emily and her bridesmaids were dressing Amy from head to toe. Incredibly, both the dress and even the shoes fit!

Amy frantically called her mother and bridesmaids on the phone to update them on her amazing day while Emily and her bridesmaids continued to dress her. As she told her mother of Emily's incredible kindness, she caught her first glimpse of herself in the beautiful dress. Amy suddenly dropped the phone and began bawling in happiness. "It was more than a miracle," says Amy. "For her to share the most important day of her life and her dress with me was the ultimate sign of sharing and caring. I couldn't stop crying I was so happy."

Amy made it to her wedding just in time for a glorious ceremony. Meanwhile Emily and Ray jumped on a plane that night to head for a romantic Hawaii honeymoon. And while the newlyweds looked lovingly into each other's eyes on the plane they couldn't stop thinking about the re- markable event that highlighted their first day married. "One thing that this definitely made me realize was I mar- ried the right woman," says Ray. "On her biggest day of her life, she was willing to make such a great sacrifice. I am proud to be her husband."

About the Author

Chris Benguhe has been a professional writer and editor for over a decade. He served as an entertainment and lifestyle writer for such high-profile publications as *People* magazine, *The National Enquirer*, and *The Globe*, where he covered many blockbuster stories during his tenure.

He has also worked as the editor-in-chief of several publications, including his own arts and entertainment magazine in Scottsdale, Arizona.

He gave up his lucrative career in national journalism to devote his life promoting positive acts through his *Triumphs of the Heart* book series as well as many other television and media projects currently in development.

Chris divides his time between his hometown of Phoenix, Arizona, and Los Angeles, California.